simple woven garments

20+ Projects to Weave & Wear

Sara Goldenberg & Jane Patrick

INTERWEAVE™
interweave.com

Editor Erica Smith
Technical Editor Judy Steinkoenig
Photographer Joe Hancock
Stylist Katie Himmelberg
Hair and Makeup Kathy MacKay
Art Director Charlene Tiedemann
Cover and Interior Design Studio Court
Production Kerry Jackson

Interweave
A division of F+W Media, Inc.
4868 Innovation Drive
Fort Collins, CO 80525-5576
interweave.com

Manufactured in China by
RR-Donnelley Shenzhen

Library of Congress
Cataloging-in-Publication Data

Goldenberg, Sara.
  Simple woven style : 20+ garments to
weave & wear / Sara Goldenberg and
Jane Patrick.
    pages cm
  Includes bibliographical references.
ISBN 978-1-62033-617-5 (pbk.)
ISBN 978-1-62033-552-9 (PDF)
 1. Knitting. 2. Sweaters. 3. Shawls.
I. Goldenberg, Sara.
II. Title.
  TT825.P377 2015
  746.43'2--dc23

2014028515

10 9 8 7 6 5 4 3 2 1

ACKNOWLEDGMENTS

We'd like to thank these generous yarn companies for providing us with yarn for some of our designs: Alpaca Fiber Cooperative of North America, Berroco, Brown Sheep Company, Classic Elite Yarns, EmmaCreation, Interlacements Yarns, Isager, Koigu Wool Designs, Lorna's Laces, Louet North America, Mountain Colors Yarns, Mountain Meadow Wool, Plymouth Yarn Company, Prism Yarns, Shibui Knits, Skacel, SweetGeorgia Yarns, Tahki-Stacy Charles Inc./ Filatura Di Crosa, Trendsetter Yarns, Universal Yarn, and WEBS/ Valley Fibers.

Many thanks to our summer intern David Pipinich who did much sampling and weaving (thanks, too, to Professor Tom Lundberg of CSU for sending him). Thanks to Judy Pagels and Nancy McRay for contributing designs. Thanks to Schacht Spindle Company for hiring our intern and for supplying all the equipment used in this volume (full disclosure: Jane's husband is Barry Schacht, founder of Schacht Spindle Company and a big supporter of our book project). We appreciate Betty Paepke and Gail Matthews for pitching in with weaving assistance. A most grateful thanks to Ryan, Blanche, and Steve for helping care for adorable baby Sylvia as the deadline pressed.

And last but not least, a heartfelt thank-you to Interweave for believing in this project.

CONTENTS

INTRODUCTION

We wanted to write this book because we think new weavers (and experienced ones, too) are ready to launch into garment making. We thought that by providing some appealing designs that are easy to weave and sew, we could offer the information you need to create garments on your own with confidence.

All of these garments are made from simple designs. In designing each garment, we considered both the fabric and the garment construction. First, we wanted to design a fabric that worked for the intended use. And second, we strove to design garments that require simple construction and no buttonholes or zippers. You don't have to be a couture seamstress to sew these garments.

We know that it is a tricky and sometimes frightening thing to cut into your precious handwoven fabric. What if I cut in the wrong place? What if the fabric ravels? What if the garment doesn't work? We kept these questions in mind as we planned the projects. We also hope that we've provided all the supplementary information you'll need to weave and sew with self-assurance.

We've assumed that you know how to warp your loom and have a bit of weaving experience. The reader we have in mind is one who is an advanced beginner to expert weaver, knits a lot or a little, and knows how to sew a seam on a sewing machine.

We haven't labeled the projects as rigid-heddle or shaft loom, but we have sampled and woven projects on both rigid-heddle and shaft looms. Our goal was to make the projects approachable for either kind of loom, and we have tested projects to the point that we feel confident that these pieces can be woven on either a shaft or rigid-heddle loom.

Sara is an expert and experienced sewer, and I can barely sew a seam. Our litmus test was: "If Jane can sew it, anyone can." This directed much of the garment design. You'll find that most garments have very few pieces and seams. Only two projects have any serious amount of sewing and even then the sewing is "Jane proof." To add shaping, we sometimes used knitting—collars, cuffs, and at the waist. We also employed some weaving techniques, such as pulled warps or sewing in a drawstring, to add shaping at the shoulders and waist.

You'll find a broad range of yarns, primarily knitting yarns, in the projects. Even though it is often stated that you can't use knitting yarns for weaving, we were quite successful with all of the yarns used here. We would broadly say that when using knitting yarns for weaving, you need to be aware that some yarns are going to have a lot of stretch. Because there is less tension on a rigid-heddle loom, the stretchiness of a yarn is not as important a consideration as when using the same yarn on a shaft loom.

We have had a blast working on this book together, and we hope that these ideas will spark your own and launch you on a mission to weave, weave, weave.

ON OUR COLLABORATION

It is joyous to collaborate on a project. But to be fully harmonious, the parties must be able to have honest discourse, like each other, live up to their part of the project (pull their own weight), and trust and respect each other. Having a similar vision and aesthetic doesn't hurt, either. If what I've just said is true, and in regard to this project I'd say it is, then creating a book together is a special and wonderful experience indeed.

It has been especially fun to work with Sara, even thrilling from time to time when we shared an idea or clipping from a magazine to find that we were both tracking along the exact same lines. Sara has lent her sense of style and design to the creation of these garments, as well as her sewing expertise. She comes with credentials, too: an MFA in fibers from CSU in Fort Collins, Colorado. Sara is an exhibited artist, and many of her forms are sculptural—which helps when thinking about designing for the body. Her art training in both sculpture and textiles shines through in the way she masters form and color.

I've lent years of weaving as well as my experience as a past editor of *Handwoven*— which is where I learned so much from the magazine's contributors—truly deepening my weaving vocabulary in profound ways. I've also been responsible for the writing and material development for this book.

I first met Sara when she was a student at CSU. I had contacted her professor, Tom Lundberg, looking for a summer intern. He sent me Sara, in part because she also lived in Boulder. Even though Sara was busy with her master's studies, she agreed to work with me every morning for a summer. Spending that much time with a person could be a trial, but our working together was most compatible and pleasurable. I really loved working with Sara, and I think she felt the same way about working with me. When I thought of the idea of making this book, I knew Sara was the one to make it happen.

From both of us, we hope you'll soon be wearing something handwoven, inspired by what you find herein.

Jane Patrick

HOW TO USE THIS BOOK

We've organized the projects loosely by difficulty, beginning with our V Shawl, which is just two rectangles sewn together at right angles, and ending with our Swing Top, a design that requires cutting, shaping, and sewing of several pieces. In between are mostly rectangles sewn together into a variety of configurations or embellished in some way such as sewing a long ruffled strip around the sides of a rectangle for our Starry, Starry Night Shawl.

Each project includes an overview and complete weaving, finishing, and assembly instructions, as well as assembly illustrations and ideas for interpreting a project in other ways. While we've given particular instructions for the designs shown, we also want you to feel free to vary our ideas to create your own unique wearables.

SHAPING

Even though some garments (such as the Green-Gray Topper) are merely connected rectangles without any additional shaping, some pieces (such as the Cowl-Neck Sweater) use knitted trims to give shape. Another technique we've employed several times—and it always looks trickier than it is—is to gather the fabric by pulling a thread. You'll find a hint of this in the Swing Top and a long stretch of gathered fabric on the Ruffled Shawl. A similar effect is achieved by threading a drawstring through the fabric after weaving to gather the cloth as in the Flame Lace Top.

Another trick we employed is using pleats to add shape. You'll find single pleats across the shoulders in our Sweater Jacket and accordion pleats around the neckline of our Cape with Collar. There's a lovely box pleat in the back of our Swing Top that just makes the design pop. You can intentionally plan for pleats as a way to add shape to your garment, or use them when a little fullness needs to be removed or to adjust sizing.

We've assumed that you are a weaver first and a stitcher second. Therefore, we avoided zippers, buttonholes, and garments with many pieces. If you think that a rectangle can be tapered or gathered or cut into for a neck hole, you can visualize all kinds of garments made from the fabric of your own creation.

SELVEDGES ARE YOUR FRIENDS

We've made extensive use of selvedges whenever possible. Because these edges are in a way prefinished, you don't have to worry about raveling. When we did cut into fabric, we always used zigzag stitch first on either side of the cutting line or at the end of the fabric before cutting off any warp ends.

ABOUT THE DRAFTS

We designed these garments knowing that our readers may want to weave them on either a shaft loom or a rigid-heddle loom. We are therefore including weaving drafts for any project that requires a pick-up stick pattern. The drafts are all written for rising-shed looms. That is, what is noted in the tie-up box is for the threads that will be lifted. Therefore, it follows that the treadling denotes which weft threads are passing under which warps. The threading reads right to left, and the treadling reads top to bottom.

We've limited the maximum warp width to 25" (63.5 cm), making every project weavable on a rigid-heddle loom. Additionally, our finest sett is 24 ends per inch, which requires two 12-dent heddles if weaving on a rigid-heddle loom. However, most of our setts are at 5, 8, 10, or 12 ends per inch (epi).

DOUBLED THREADS

For several projects, we've doubled the threads in either warp or weft. Doubling is a way to use a fine yarn at a larger sett. For example, instead of setting a yarn at 16 ends per inch, you can double it and weave the fabric at 8 ends per inch. We've noted when a yarn has been doubled. We've given the actual number of threads measured, because you will need to measure that many for your project. The doubled threads will act as one in the weaving. For example, let's say the pattern calls for 20 actual ends and 10 working ends: this means that you will measure 20 ends but double them in the heddle or reed, filling 10 spaces.

Should threads be doubled in the weft, you will just wind them together on the shuttle.

SHAFT LOOM VERSUS RIGID-HEDDLE LOOM

If you're a new weaver, chances are you started weaving on a rigid-heddle loom. You may still be weaving on this delightful little loom, and you could weave every project in this book on one if you wanted to. Here are some considerations:

▸ *Weaving speed.* Because you use your feet for making the sheds, you can weave faster on a shaft loom.

▸ *Warping speed.* Whether you direct-peg warp or measure your yarn on a warping board first, you'll be up and weaving sooner on a rigid-heddle loom than on a shaft loom.

▸ *Warp length.* We have warped as much as 6 yards (5.5 m) on a Flip rigid-heddle loom. We rolled on with brown packing paper—if you use something thicker, you probably won't be able to wind that much warp on. The length of the warp that the beams on a rigid-heddle loom will accommodate is related to the thickness of the yarn (as well as the thickness of the paper you wind on with). You'll need a little over 5 yards (4.5 m) for the Good Earth Ruana, but the thickness of the yarns will create a roll that is too large. So when weaving this project on a rigid-heddle loom or a table loom, you'll need to weave two separate warps, one for each side of the garment. The warp length will not be a problem if you're weaving on a shaft loom.

▸ *Tension.* Even though you can crank up the tension quite tightly on a rigid-heddle loom, you'll never achieve the same amount as you can achieve on a shaft loom. This isn't bad or good, just different. The same yarn with the same sett will pack in more on the shaft loom. To compensate, just use a lighter beat when weaving on a shaft loom. Because the warp yarn is not stretched as far or as tightly on a rigid-heddle loom, you can actually get away with using more delicate yarns on the rigid-heddle loom than you can on a shaft loom—an advantage if it is an expensive or delicate yarn.

▸ *Loom waste.* We generally figure 24" (61 cm) for a rigid-heddle or table loom. For a shaft loom, you'll generally need to allow 36" (91.5 cm).

HEMSTITCHING

Hemstitching is a great weft protector and edge finish for a garment with a fringed edge. It is easy to do on the loom when the weaving is under tension. These instructions are written working right to left, but if you are left-handed, you may find it more comfortable to work left to right. Hemstitching is a two-part stitch, and once you have the hang of it, it progresses smoothly. Here, we've shown hemstitching at the beginning of the weaving. At the end of the weaving, you will again work right to left, but you will stitch down into the fabric as opposed to up into the fabric as illustrated here.

Step 1: Begin by leaving a tail at the right side, 3 to 4 times longer than the width of your weaving.

Step 2: Weave at least 3 to 5 rows of plain weave.

Step 3: Thread a tapestry needle with the tail and work on a closed shed.

Step 4: Beginning at the right selvedge, insert the needle diagonally right to left under 3 warp ends and up 3 weft ends. Bring the needle to the surface, pulling the yarn through (**Figure 1**).

Step 5: Place the needle horizontally along the edge of the weaving, under the same 3 warp threads. The needle should be over the working end so that it is caught to encircle these threads (**Figure 2**).

Step 6: Pull tight up and back toward the weaving. Repeat all the way across (**Figure 3**). Sew the tail into the weaving to secure the end.

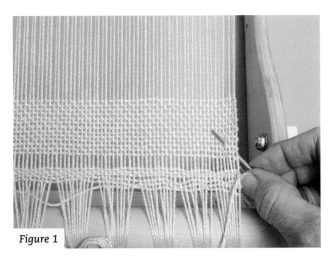
Figure 1

Figure 2

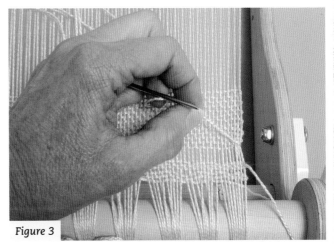
Figure 3

USING TWO SHUTTLES

When weaving with two shuttles, you need to interlock the wefts at the selvedge. Which side you start on and whether your selvedge thread is up or down will determine how the interlock happens. Here, the selvedge threads are threaded in holes. The interlock happens naturally depending on how the shuttles are placed after each pass.

Step 1: Place the heddle in the up position and weave across. The pink weft is over the yellow one and will lock it in automatically. Change sheds (heddle in down position).

Step 2: Weave across. So that wefts automatically interlock, always place the following shuttle farthest away from you. The first shuttle will always be closest to you.

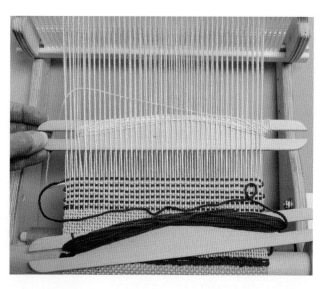

FINISHING

As one of our weaving teachers used to say, "It's not finished until it's finished." Every fabric that comes off the loom will not achieve its full potential until it's finished. Depending on the fabric and the desired result, finishing may involve handwashing, air-drying, and a good pressing. Or, as in the case of our tabard, the fabric may be thrown into the washing machine and given a vigorous felted finish. We've noted our finishing process in the instructions with each project. Our advice: When in doubt, do a mild finish. You can always do more, but never less.

ON MEASURING

Making a garment requires measuring, and this begins with your sample. First, weave a sample that is large enough to give you the best idea of how your fabric will behave in the final garment. Generally, you'll want to warp at least 8" (20.5 cm) wide and weave 20" (51 cm) long to determine how much your cloth will draw in weftwise, take-up warpwise, and shrink in the finishing process. The more accurate you are with your sample, the more reliable your information.

For a rigid heddle loom, putting on about 1½ yards (1.3 m) is about the minimum for a sample. On a shaft loom, about 2 yards (1.8 m) is the minimum required for sampling.

As you weave, measure your picks per inch off-tension (with no tension on the fabric). Write down this number (we recall many painful memories of failing to do this). When you remove the weaving from the loom, measure the width and length. Also, to really know how much take-up you have, measure all of your loom waste and make a note of it. Finish the sample until you have the hand you want for your finished garment. Be sure to write the measurements down. Now you'll need to do the math to determine how much yardage you'll need for your finished project.

Of course, you can dispense with all of the above if you follow the instructions for the garments in this book—we've done this work for you. However, if you substitute yarns, our advice is to *make a sample*.

WHAT IS MY YARDAGE PER POUND?

If you want to substitute a yarn from your stash but don't know how much you have, you can figure this by doing a little math if you know the put-up of the yarn you want to use.

Let's say the yarn has 180 yd in 4.5 oz tubes. To figure out how many yards per pound the yarn yields, work this simple equation (see illustration). Multiply 180 × 16 = 2,880 and divide this number by 4.5 to yield 640 yd/lb.

$$\frac{180 \text{ yd}}{4.5 \text{ oz}} = \frac{? \text{ yd}}{16 \text{ oz}}$$

You can then compare this yardage with the yarn you want to substitute to see if it is similar as well as comparing this yarn with the yarn in the yarn chart (see pages 142–148).

Once you're pretty sure the yarn will work, you're not finished yet. We always, always, always weave a sample. We're not sure why people seem to be so adverse to sample weaving, but it really is the only way to truly know for sure that you're going to get the result you're aiming for.

HOW MUCH YARN DO I HAVE?

One of the tricky things in planning projects from your stash is deciding if you have enough yarn for the project. You can always take your chances by eyeballing the yarn and guessing at the quantity. However, if you want to know for sure, you can use a Yarn Yardage Counter to determine the yardage. This simple tool weighs a length of the yarn that you want to use, and with some calculations, you can determine the yardage per pound.

Finding yards per pound using a yarn balance

Step 1: Balance the pin of the balance arm in the slots on the sides of the balance.

Step 2: Place a length of yarn in the notch of the arm.

Step 3: Cut the yarn little by little until the arm is balanced.

Step 4: Measure this length of yarn on a ruler. Multiply by 100 to get the total yards per pound.

Determining yarn quantity

Step 1: Use a food or mail scale to weigh the ball of yarn to find the total weight of the yarn on hand.

Step 2: To know if you have enough yarn, you need to do a little math.

In this example, the yarn yielded 15" (38 cm) in length. Multiply 15 by 100 for a total of 1,500 yd/lb. Let's say the ball of yarn when weighed yielded 4 oz (113 g). To find out how much yarn is available, use this simple equation.

First multiply 4 × 1,500 = 6,000

Divide this number by 16 to give the total amount of yarn, or 375 yd.

$$\frac{1,500 \text{ yd}}{16 \text{ oz}} = \frac{? \text{ yd}}{4 \text{ oz}}$$

▲ Yarn balance

▲ Determine yarn quantity

SEWING

Making a double rolled hem

Because a rolled hem gives such a tidy and secure finish to the edge of a handwoven fabric, we've used it a lot in this book. The width of the rolled hem varies and is determined by the bulk of the fabric. The bulkier the fabric, the wider the hem.

Make a rolled hem by folding the edge over twice, giving the cloth a clean, stable edge. Be sure that the initial fold of the cloth is the same width all the way across the fabric (**Figure 1**). Having a small metal ruler handy is helpful for checking the width.

Steam-press the first fold into place. Check the width as you press (a metal ruler is nice because it will not melt near the iron!). The width of the initial fold determines the width of the hem. A ¼" (6 mm) initial fold will create a ¼" (6 mm) hem. Once the initial fold is steam-pressed into place, fold the fabric over once more so that the raw edge is tucked into the hem. Use the first fold as the guide for the second fold. Follow the edge of the first fold the length of the fabric (**Figure 2**) and steam-press the second fold. Pin the hem into place and hand or machine stitch. For slippery or dense cloth, hand basting before machine stitching is helpful. Stitch the hem slowly, making sure the fabric isn't bunching. Backstitch at the beginning and end of the hem.

▲ **Figure 1** The initial fold.

▲ **Figure 2** The second fold, pinned.

Zigzag stitching

The zigzag stitch is very important when making garments from handwoven cloth. Before you cut your cloth, always zigzag on either side of your cutting line to prevent raveling. If you're zigzagging a thick fabric, increase the zigzag width on your sewing machine so that the width of the fabric isn't stretched out or pulled in. Doing a small test first on scrap fabric is helpful.

Stitch length

Different yarns require different stitch lengths. For thin yarns, use a shorter stitch length and for thick yarns, a longer stitch length. It is always helpful to do a small test on a scrap bit of woven cloth for each garment to find the stitch length that allows the cloth to lie flat. If a stitch length is too long or too short, the fabric can draw in or splay out.

Stitching ribbon yarns

Stitching ribbon yarn can be tricky because it has a tendency to be drawn down into the sewing machine. To prevent snags, stitch very slowly on all ribbon areas whether using a zigzag or straight stitch.

Needles and oiling

Always make sure you are using a sharp needle; dull needles can cause unwanted snags in your handwovens. Also, be sure to keep your machine oiled; dry machines can cause bobbin tension issues.

Backstitching

A backstitch is a useful handstitch for sewing a seam or attaching two pieces of fabric because it gives a continuous line, unlike a running stitch.

Step 1: Insert needle into cloth and come back up to the top surface (**Figure 1**).

Step 2: For the next stitch, insert your needle back toward the stitching and come up in front of the last stitch (**Figure 2**). Repeat.

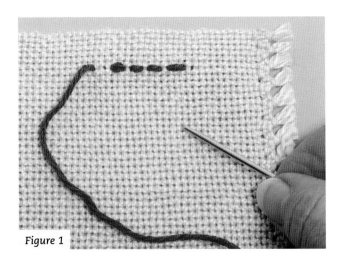
Figure 1

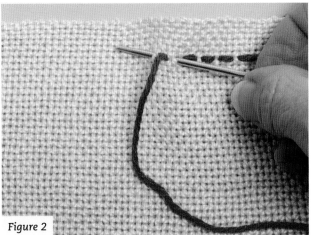
Figure 2

CUTTING

When it comes down to cutting, as they say in the woodworking field: measure twice, cut once. We would say, check again! And when in doubt, make a sample out of muslin fabric and use that to check your measurements and fit. Then you'll be able to proceed with sureness.

We made muslins for every project that required cutting. We used them to test ideas, check fit, try out necklines, as well as make sure our calculations were correct. We can't urge you enough to check and double-check your measurements, and if you are nervous, it's well worth the time to cut first in muslin.

HOW TO MAKE MUSLIN PATTERNS

When trying to determine the size of a garment, muslin patterns are the best way to know for sure. Not much is worse than weaving and sewing a piece and ending up with an ill-fitting garment. Making a muslin, like knitting up a gauge swatch, lets you proceed with confidence.

Muslin fabric is perfect for this task because it is affordable and drapes well. Another bonus of using muslin is that you can take notes with a pen or pencil right on the cloth.

If you are wondering how wide or how long your woven fabric should be for your intended garment, make a muslin pattern first before purchasing your yarn and setting up the loom.

Most patterns in this book allow for ½" (1.3 cm) or ⅝" (1.5 cm) seam allowances, so be sure to check the seam allowance for the project and use that same amount when cutting and making your pattern.

When making a pattern for a garment, it's a good idea to start big and trim off any excess. This way, you don't have to start all over if the pattern is too small. However, when determining the sizing of the neck hole, err on the smaller side because you can always cut more cloth away for a bigger opening.

When constructing the muslin, pin the pieces together first, instead of stitching, so that you can make size adjustments by repositioning the pins.

Many of the garments in this book are made by connecting two rectangles. When cutting the muslin to make your pattern, be sure that the pieces are squared so you get an accurate sense of how the garment will go together. Rotary cutters and healing mats are great for accurate cutting. Also, be sure to iron out any creases or crinkles before making the pattern. After you are satisfied that the pattern size is accurate, stitch the pieces together using a long stitch on the sewing machine or hand baste, in case you need to rip anything out.

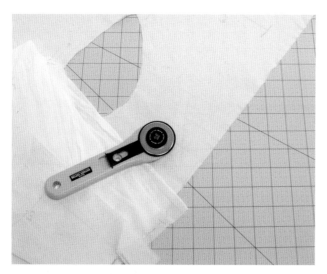

▲ Use muslin fabric to cut pattern pieces to check fit and sizing. A rotary cutter and a healing mat are helpful tools.

CUTTING NECK HOLES

Cutting neck holes is probably the most stressful part of making any of these garments. After spending so much time creating the cloth, cutting a large hole in the center of your weaving is a bit nerve-racking! The best way to reduce stress is to first make a muslin mock-up before cutting the neck hole in the actual garment. When cutting a neck hole in a handwoven fabric for the first time, do a test run on a scrap piece of handwoven cloth to get comfortable with the process.

Create a template. Draw the template for a V-neck, round neck or square neck on a piece of paper (**Figure 1**), then trace the shape onto muslin. Cut a square or rectangular piece of muslin that is at least 3" to 4" (7.5 to 10 cm) wider than the neck hole on all sides. Cut out the muslin along the traced line. Then try it on and see what you think. If it's too small, cut away extra cloth. Be sure to keep accurate measurements so you can create a new paper template.

Guidelines for neck-hole templates are given, but you may find that you prefer a larger or smaller neck hole. Don't worry about creating hems on the muslin mock-up. Just cut the neck opening to the desired size. Once you have found the perfect neck shape for your piece, lay your paper template out on the woven cloth. The placement of the neck hole will vary from piece to piece. Most neck holes are offset toward the front of the garment. Pin the template onto the woven cloth and either zigzag or straight stitch around the template (**Figure 2**—refer to instructions for specific garments). Straight stitching around the template works well on fine fibers but not so well on thick fiber where a zigzag stitch is recommended.

Unless you are looking for a raw-edge neck hole, you will need to create 2 rows of securing stitches before cutting anything out of the garment. *Do not* cut after stitching a single securing edge around the template.

For thick fabric, move into the center of the neckhole 1" (2.5 cm) from the first row of stitching and stitch a second securing row (**Figure 3**). For finer fabrics, ½" (1.3 cm) will be enough. The cloth between the 2 securing rows will be used for a rolled hem to add stability to the neck-hole opening and to prevent raveling.

The diagrams in this book show snip lines on all neck holes. Stitch with a straight stitch directly on either side of your snip lines (**Figure 4**). Make sure you stitch all areas of the neck hole before any cutting occurs.

Once all of the neck-hole stitching is complete, cut out the centermost area of the neck opening (**Figure 5**). Be sure to leave all stitch lines intact. Once the inner portion of the neck hole is cut out, snip between securing stitches (**Figure 6**). Use very sharp scissors and stop your snip ⅛" (3 mm) before the outermost securing stitch line. Securing around the snip lines is very important, or else the fabric will ravel.

Now there will be multiple flaps of fabric; the number will vary with the size and style of neck hole (three for a V-neck and four for a square neck, for example). On the wrong side of the fabric, create double rolled hems making the initial fold by folding the edge of the cloth until it butts up against the outermost securing stitch line. Steam-press and then fold over once more so that the securing line is seen on the wrong side of the cloth and not the front of your garment. Steam-press once more, pin, and stitch into place. It is helpful to hand baste before sewing on the sewing machine. It is much easier to baste first than it is to rip out stitches later!

USING A TEMPLATE TO CREATE A NECK-HOLE

Figure 1

TEMPLATE
6" (15 cm)

Draw the template on a piece of paper, then trace the shape onto muslin.

Figure 2

GARMENT

Zigzag stitch around the outside of the template

Figure 3

GARMENT

Remove template and zigzag stitch inside the last zigzag stitching.

Figure 4

GARMENT

------- = straight stitch
wwww = zigzag stitch

Machine straight stitch on either side of the snip line.

Figure 5

GARMENT

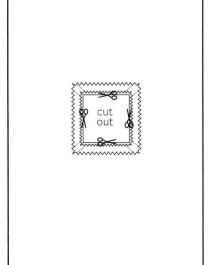

cut out

Cut out the center of the neckline inside the innermost zigzag stitching.

Figure 6

GARMENT

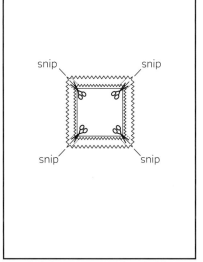

snip   snip

snip   snip

Snip between straight stitching within ⅛" (3 mm) of outer most zigzag stitching.

ON SIZING

Making a muslin pattern directly correlates to determining sizing. We will use three projects from the book to illustrate how to figure out size. We have chosen one boatneck piece, one tunic, and one long-sleeved garment.

First, find your measurements. Measure your wingspan from palm to palm, bust at its fullest point, waist at its narrowest point, hips at widest point, circumference of bicep and wrist, and torso length (by measuring on the back from the top of the shoulder to the hip and from the top of the shoulder to the waist). Keep these measurements on hand. Not all measurements are needed for each project.

Fit and construction of boatneck tops

Boatneck tops are versatile in fit and easy to construct. They are made by sewing two rectangles together, leaving a neck-hole area unsewn, and sewing up the side seams. The length of each piece of fabric is determined by how long you want the sides to drape over the shoulders. Presuming that you are not adding knitted trims to the sleeves, determine the size of the panels by measuring across the back from mid bicep to mid bicep or from underarm to underarm. One results in a shorter sleeve and the other produces a longer sleeve, respectively. The width of the panel (which is how long the panel will be when used sideways) is determined by measuring from the top of the shoulder, over the bust, to the waist or hip, depending on where you want the garment to fall. To check fit, cut two

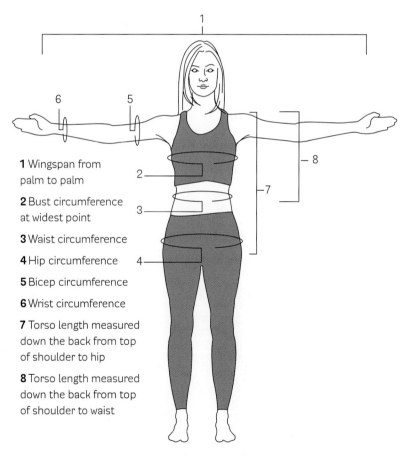

1 Wingspan from palm to palm

2 Bust circumference at widest point

3 Waist circumference

4 Hip circumference

5 Bicep circumference

6 Wrist circumference

7 Torso length measured down the back from top of shoulder to hip

8 Torso length measured down the back from top of shoulder to waist

TAKING YOUR MEASUREMENTS

rectangles out of muslin using your dimensions plus seam allowances. If you want to experiment with the fit of the neck hole, cut the rectangles larger at first and trim down if necessary.

Note: In determining the garment dimensions, remember that these dimensions are for the finished fabric and do not take into account draw-in and take-up or shrinkage during the finishing process. These figures will vary depending on the yarn, fiber, and finishing process. When making yarn substitutions, our advice is to always do a sample first.

Long turtleneck tunic

Another versatile muslin pattern to create is for a long tunic. For the boatneck top, two rectangles are connected horizontally. For the tunic, two rectangles are connected vertically. Alternately, a neck hole can be cut out of one long length of cloth. With either construction, the side seams will need to be sewn.

To determine the length of your tunic, measure from the top of the shoulder down the back with a soft measuring tape, stopping at the hip (depending on the garment style, you can always add or subtract length). This length plus the seam allowance needed for the shoulder seams and any hems at the bottom will be the length of your rectangles.

If no shoulder seams are required, take the top of the shoulder to hip measurement, multiply by two, and add hem length to determine the length for your fabric.

To find the width of your tunic, measure around your hips and bust and add 3" (7.5 cm) to the widest measurement. Next, add seam allowances for both side seams, divide this number by two, and you will have the width of your rectangles. Note that you can always cut the rectangles a bit larger and trim them down later if necessary.

How to measure for the hoodie and/or Ode to Coco jacket

These two garments start with two rectangles. The length of each rectangle should be 4" (10 cm) less than your wingspan. Both pieces have cuffs to add the extra length needed. To determine the width of your cloth, measure down from the top of your shoulder

to the waist allowing the tape measure to drape over the bust. Take this measurement and add extra width for draw-in and seam allowances. Cut two rectangles using these two dimensions.

Next, you will need your hip measurement to figure out how wide the body of the sweater and/or jacket should be. Add 6" (15 cm) to your hip measurement and divide this number by two. This will be the width of each panel up the torso to the armpit, where the sleeve begins.

Ode to Coco cuffs

The edge of the sleeve starts at the armpit and will be the widest point, tapering down to the wrist. Use your bicep measurement to determine the widest point of your sleeve. Take your bicep measurement, multiply by 1.5, and divide this number by two for the total width needed for each panel, including seam allowances for the widest part of the arm. Taper slowly down to the wrist. Determine your wrist circumference by doing the same thing as with the bicep measurement, but with the distance around your wrist, always measure loosely. Again the number will include the seam allowance.

This way of determining size makes for a relaxed fit. For something tighter in the body or arm, adjust down, or for something with a bit more room, adjust the numbers up. The hoodie arms are tighter than the sleeves of the Ode to Coco jacket, for example.

PATTERNS USING PICK-UP STICKS

Because of its unique design, the rigid-heddle loom is especially suited for pick-up patterns. If you look at your heddle on the loom, you can see that when it is in the down position, the slot threads are up. When the heddle is in the up position, the hole threads are up, and when the heddle is in neutral, no threads are raised or lowered. It is the slot threads' ability to move freely that allows them to be easily picked up. Likewise, it is good to remember that the hole threads are fixed.

Weaving pick-up patterns requires a pick-up stick or two. We like our pick-up sticks to be a few inches longer than the weaving is wide. For example, if the warp is 20" (51 cm) wide, choose a 25" (63.5 cm) pick-up stick so that you can hold onto it on either side. Pick-up sticks come in a variety of widths. We like one that is at least 1" (2.5 cm) wide. The wider the pick-up stick, the bigger your shed will be. We also prefer pick-up sticks with tapered points and flat, not curved edges.

The first step in weaving pick-up patterns is to place the heddle in the down position. This will raise the slot threads. The pick-up stick is used behind the heddle (between the heddle and the back of the loom) and picks up only the raised threads. To separate the layers, you may find it helpful to place a piece of narrow cardboard or paper between the two layers. If you are still having trouble seeing behind the heddle, you can do the pick-up in front of the heddle and then transfer the pattern to a second pick-up stick behind the heddle (remove the first pick-up stick after the threads are transferred). Or alternately, as we've done here, turn the loom around and pick up the threads from the back of the loom. *Note: If you begin the pick-up from the left side, when you turn the loom around, the pattern will start on the right side (as if you've threaded from the front of the loom, right to left).*

To pick up threads, with the heddle in the down position, place some raised threads on the pick-up stick and not others. For example, in a 1 up, 1 down pattern, you would pick up every other thread *on the raised threads only* (**Figure 1**). The bottom layer doesn't factor into picking up the threads at all.

Once you have the desired threads picked up, slide the pick-up stick to the back until you need it (**Figure 2**). Remove the paper if you used it to divide the layers.

Your pick-up stick can be used to create either warp or weft floats (threads that float over more than one thread). It just depends on how you use it. To weave weft floats, place the heddle in neutral and bring the pick-up stick forward to just behind the heddle and *turn it on edge* (**Figure 3**). You have now created a third shed. For this example, picking 1 up, 1 down, you'll notice that the weft travels over three warps and under one, and so on.

Without changing the picked-up pattern on the pick-up stick, you can weave warp floats. Place the heddle in the up position and slide the pick-up stick forward

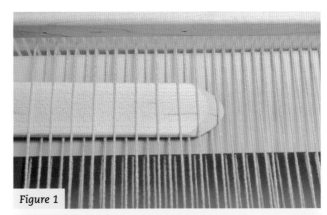
Figure 1

Figure 2

Figure 3

Figure 4

to behind the heddle without turning it on edge (*leave it flat*). Look into the shed from the side as you slide the pick-up stick toward the heddle (**Figure 4**). You'll see that this draws up the warp threads from the bottom of the shed to the top of the shed to make warp floats.

These two possibilities provide endless variations in how threads are either picked up or woven in combination with plain weave.

Pick-up patterns are read like this

Pick-up pattern: 1 up, 1 down (heddle is in down position; every other raised thread is picked up on the top layer only).

Weaving weft floats might look like this

Step 1: Up (heddle in up position), weave across. Beat.

Step 2: Pick-up stick (heddle in the neutral position, turn the pick-up stick on edge) and weave across. Beat. Then, slide the pick-up stick to the back of the loom until it is needed again.

Step 3: Up (heddle in up position), weave across. Beat.

Step 4: Down (heddle in down position), weave across. Beat.

Repeat this pattern.

Weaving warp floats might look like this

Step 1: Down (heddle in down position), weave across. Beat.

Step 2: Up and pick-up stick (heddle in up position, slide pick-up stick flat up to the heddle), weave across. Beat. Slide the pick-up stick to the back of the loom until it is needed again.

Step 3: Down (heddle in down position), weave across. Beat.

Step 4: Up (heddle in up position), weave across. Beat.

Repeat this pattern.

See *The Weaver's Idea Book* for more pick-up explorations.

PULLING THREADS TO ADD SHAPING

Handwoven fabric is ideal for shaping by pulling threads. You can either pull them warpwise or weftwise, depending on the application. For example, we pulled warp threads to shape the ruffled trim for the Ruffled Shawl; we gathered weft threads for the Flame Lace Top.

Tip: If pulling a laid-in yarn, you'll want to knot it at the other end so it doesn't pull through the fabric.

All that's involved in pulling a thread is to pull one or two yarns and spread out the gathered area evenly along the length of the fabric being gathered (**Figure 1**).

Figure 1

KNITTING: HOW TO PICK UP STITCHES ALONG A WOVEN EDGE

Use a crochet hook to pick up stitches along the woven edge. Be sure to leave 2 to 3 rows of woven cloth along the edge where stitches are picked up. *Note: Picking up too close to the zigzag stitching securing the edge puts too much strain on the stitching and can cause the stitches to come out.*

Use a crochet hook that is either the same size as the knitting needle or one size smaller. Pull the yarn from the wrong side of the fabric to the front side. Leave a long tail on the end of the first stitch pulled through. This tail will be sewn into the garment. Transfer stitches from the crochet hook to the knitting needle every three to five stitches. Be mindful that the loops on the knitting needle are of even tension.

Also be sure that the stitches are picked up the same distance from the edge of the cloth all the way around, or across the woven edge. You may find it helpful to mark the pick-up line with pins.

Step 1: Leave a long tail to be sewn in later.

Step 2: Using a crochet hook, begin at the edge of the fabric and pick up stitches 2 to 3 rows from the edge of the fabric; here we've shown the selvedge edge (**Figure 1**).

Step 3: Poke the crochet hook from the right side to the wrong side and draw a loop through. Skip at least 2 threads and repeat (**Figure 2**).

Step 4: When there are three to five loops on the crochet hook, transfer to a knitting needle. Repeat (**Figure 3**).

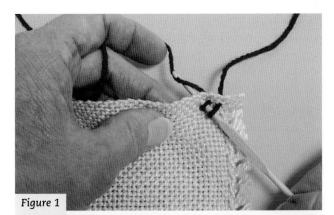

Figure 1

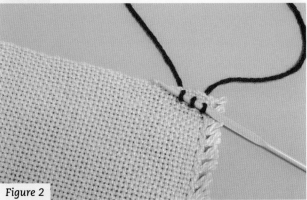

Figure 2

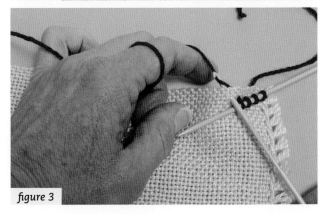

figure 3

Have fun exploring color-and-weave effect with this V shawl. Each panel is woven in a different pattern, making this piece a delight to weave. This soft chainette yarn makes for a yummy fabric and at 5 ends per inch, weaves up quickly.

V SHAWL

Designed and woven by *Sara Goldenberg*

This twist on the ubiquitous shawl is easy to weave and wear. Two panels are woven and joined in the back to form a V. You'll find that this shawl falls comfortably from the shoulders. Wear the front straight down or flip the ends back for a bit of coziness. You can also turn the shawl around, wearing the V in front and wrapping the ends around for a different look.

Garment size: One size fits all.

Finished dimensions: 13½" (34.5 cm) wide. Panel 1: 48" (122 cm) long plus 8" (20.5 cm) fringe. Panel 2: 35" (89 cm) long plus 8" (20.5 cm) fringe.

Equipment: loom with at least an 18" (45.5 cm) weaving width, 5-dent reed, 2 shuttles, sewing machine.

Warp and weft yarns: *Classic Elite Chalet* (70% baby alpaca/30% bamboo viscose at 891 yd/lb [815 m/453 g], 98 yd/1.76 oz [90 m/50 g] per ball) in color 7477, Charcoal, 169 yd (155 m) needed for warp and 115 yd (105 m) needed for weft; and 7416 Parchment, 169 yd (155 m) needed for warp and 121 yd (111 m) needed for weft. Three balls are needed of each color for both warp and weft.

Weave structure: plain weave.

Warp length: 3¾ yd (3.4 m), which includes take-up and 24" (61 cm) loom waste. If weaving on a shaft loom, allow 36" (91.5 cm) loom waste and increase warp yarn yardage by a third.

Warp width: 18" (45.5 cm).

Number of warp ends: 90.

Note: I made my guide string 142" (361 cm) long because the chainette yarn has a tendency to stretch during the winding process, and I wanted to be sure to obtain a 135" (343 cm) long warp.

EPI: 5.

PPI: 5.

Warp color order:

	15x		
Charcoal	3		45
Parchment		3	45
Total warp ends			90

WEAVING

Tie on to allow 8" (20 cm) of fringe at the beginning of the piece. Weave 2 panels following the weft color order.

Weft color order: Panel 1 (total woven length 57" [145 cm])

Step 1: Alternate 2 picks of Charcoal and 4 picks of Parchment 15 times (19" [48.5 cm]). End with 2 picks of Charcoal.

Step 2: Alternate 1 pick of Parchment and 1 pick of Charcoal (pick and pick) for 7 repeats (3" [7.5 cm]). End with 1 pick of Parchment.

Step 3: Weave 3 picks of Charcoal and 1 pick of Parchment for 21 repeats (17½" [44.5 cm]).

Step 4: Weave 1 pick of Charcoal and 3 picks of Parchment for 20 repeats (17½" [44.5 cm]).

Step 5: End the panel with 6 picks of Parchment for a double rolled hem.

Weave 1½" (3.8 cm) spacer with Parchment between panel 1 and panel 2.

Weft color order: Panel 2 (total woven length 41" [104 cm])

Step 1: Weave 3 picks of Charcoal for hem.

Step 2: Alternate 3 picks of Charcoal and 3 picks of Parchment for 13 repeats (18" [45.5 cm]). End with 3 picks Charcoal.

Step 3: Weave 2 picks of Parchment and 1 pick of Charcoal for 18 repeats (12½" [31.5 cm]). End with 2 picks of Parchment.

Step 4: Alternate 1 pick of Charcoal and 1 pick of Parchment (pick and pick) for 22 repeats (10½" [26.5 cm]).

VARIATION

Designed and woven by Sara Goldenberg
You can do a lot with just a length of fabric: Place it over your head and it's a hood; draped around the neck, it's a scarf; or pinned around the shoulders, it becomes a shawl. Yarns are Louet North America with Koigu accents around the edges.

COLOR-AND-WEAVE

By using colors in different sequences, you can create an amazing number of color-and-weave effects. This shawl is a sampler of sorts and is the tip of the iceberg for what's possible. In color-and-weave, the structure is always the same; in this case, it's plain weave (over, under, over, under). It's the color *order* that creates the pattern. It works like this: a warp thread can only be up or down; a weft thread can only be over or under. To simplify this concept, we've made a simple illustration (**Figure 1**).

You'll see that there are 2 black warps and 2 white wefts. When the first white weft goes under the first black warp, the black warp shows on the top. When the weft travels over the second black warp, the white appears on top. The opposite is true on the second row where the white weft weaves over the first black warp and under the second black warp. More patterns develop when you start mixing this up even more: alternating 2 black and 2 white warps and weaving across with 2 black and 2 white wefts, or 3 black and 1 white, or 1 black and 1 white, and so on. You can get "lost" in color-and-weave.

For a color-and-weave sampler, see *The Weaver's Idea Book,* pages 24–25.

▲ Warp: 3 Charcoal, 3 Parchment
Weft: 3 Charcoal, 1 Parchment

▲ Warp: 3 Charcoal, 3 Parchment
Weft: 1 Parchment, 1 Charcoal

▲ Warp: 3 Charcoal, 3 Parchment
Weft: 2 Charcoal, 4 Parchment

Figure 1

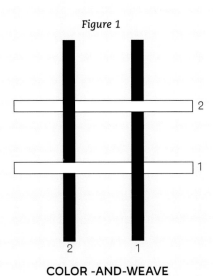

2

1

2   1

COLOR -AND-WEAVE

FABRIC FINISHING

Secure beginning and end of cloth with overhand knots, 6 ends per knot. This will become the fringe. Zigzag stitch between panel 1 and panel 2 and cut them apart. Wash by hand in hot water and mild soap with moderate agitation. To further full the fabric, place it in the dryer on medium heat with a bath towel. Keep checking every 5 minutes until sufficiently fulled. Lay flat to dry. Steam-press and trim fringe.

ASSEMBLY

On the zigzagged end, create a ½" (1.3 cm) double rolled hem on panel 1. Steam-press, pin, and stitch into place with a long stitch length on the sewing machine.

Fold the end of panel 2 under ½" (1.3 cm) at zigzag edge and steam-press. Pin panel 2 to panel 1 so that the end of panel 2 is on top of the selvedge edge of panel 1 with a ¾" (2 cm) overlap. Hand baste panels together, starting from rolled hem edge. Machine stitch with a long stitch length. Hand tack edges of panels with hems so that panels 1 and 2 flow smoothly into one another and the rolled-hem edge of panel 1 lies flat. This careful attention to detail allows the garment to be reversible. You'll notice that the color-and-weave pattern varies from front to back. Trim fringe to 8" (20.5 cm) or desired length.

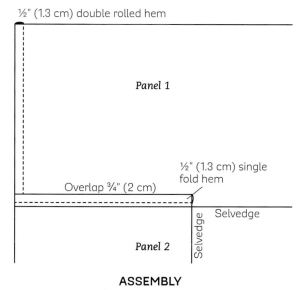

½" (1.3 cm) double rolled hem

Panel 1

½" (1.3 cm) single fold hem

Overlap ¾" (2 cm)

Selvedge

Selvedge

Panel 2

ASSEMBLY

Other fabric ideas

▶ For this type of garment, you want a fabric that has some weight to it but is not so heavy that it is stiff. This chainette yarn is ideal for this fabric and comes in lovely natural shades as well as a pastel color palette. Try an oversized check in off-white and tan for a sporty look, or try an all-white version, using a cream white for the warp and a white for the weft for an elegant result.

▶ Have fun with pattern and color by weaving one side of the V in bright stripes and crossing the stripes for a plaid on the other panel.

▶ Weave with a finer wool in an open weave and heavily full the fabric for a dense and warm shawl. Take inspiration from Scottish plaids for a traditional look.

Alternate styles

▶ Wear the V over one shoulder and throw the ends across each other.

▶ For a dramatic effect, throw one end of the shawl over the shoulder. If desired, secure with a large decorative pin.

We love things that look more complicated than they really are. This Ruffled Shawl is one such example. It's just a long piece of fabric with a second gathered piece sewn along one long edge and both ends. To make the ruffled trim, 2 warp threads were pulled along one side of the trim fabric to gather it. Wear the ruffles on the inside or out . . . it's a most flexible piece that is sure to turn heads.

RUFFLED SHAWL

Designed and woven by *Sara Goldenberg*

This project requires two warps. The first instructions are for the body of the shawl, and the second are for the ruffle. We've combined the weaving and finishing notes for both pieces.

Body of Shawl

Garment size: one size fits all.

Equipment: loom with 20" (51 cm) weaving width, 8-dent reed, 1 shuttle, sewing machine.

Finished dimensions: 17½" (44.5 cm) wide by 82" (208 cm) long.

Warp yarn: *SweetGeorgia Merino Silk Aran* (50% merino wool/50% silk at 840 yd/lb [768 m/453 g], 185 yd/3.52 oz [169 m/100 g] per skein) in Cypress, 120 yd (110 m) or 1 skein needed; and Cayenne, 360 yd (329 m) or 2 skeins needed.

Weft yarn: *Merino Silk Fine* (50% merino wool/50% silk at 1,727 yd/lb [1,579 m/453 g], 380 yd/3.52 oz [347 m/100 g] per skein) in Autumn Flame, 400 yd (366 m) or 2 skeins needed.

Weave structure: plain weave.

Warp length: 3 yd (2.75 m), which includes take-up and allows for 24" (61 cm) loom waste. If weaving on a shaft loom, allow 36" (91.5 cm) for loom waste and increase warp yarn yardage by a third.

Warp width: 20" (51 cm).

Number of warp ends: 160.

EPI: 8.

PPI: 8.

Warp color order for Body of Shawl:

		2x									
		4x			4x			8x			
Cayenne	16		1		1		40		1	24	120
Cypress		1		8		1		1			40
										Total warp ends	160

Note: Because you will be threading Cayenne and Cypress alternately, we suggest you measure the warp on a warping board. If you use the peg warping method, you will need to shift the yarns around in the heddle to achieve the color order.

WEAVING

Weave with Autumn Flame using an even beat and moderate tension to mitigate excessive take-up (this yarn has a lot of spring). Weave 84" (213 cm) or to the end of the warp.

Ruffle Fabric

Finished dimensions:
4½" (11.5 cm) wide × 220" (559 cm) long.

Warp yarn: *SweetGeorgia Merino Silk Lace* (50% merino/50% silk at 3,477 yd/lb [3,179 m/453 g], 765 yd/3.52 oz [699 m/100 g] per skein) in Autumn Flame (used doubled), 576 yd [527 m] or 1 skein needed. *SweetGeorgia Merino Silk Aran* (50% merino wool/50% silk at 840 yd/lb [768 m/453 g] 185 yd/3.52 oz [169 m/100 g] per skein) in Cypress, 104 yd (95 m) or 1 skein needed.

Weft yarn: *SweetGeorgia Merino Silk Fine* (50% merino wool/50% silk at 1,727 yd/lb [1,579 m/453 g] 380 yd/3.52 [347 m/100 g] per skein) in Cayenne, 370 yd (338 m) or 1 skein needed.

Weave structure: plain weave.

Warp length: 8 yd (7.3 m), which includes take-up and 24" (61 cm) loom waste. If weaving on a shaft loom, allow 36" (91.5 cm) loom waste and increase warp yarn yardage by a third.

Warp width: 5¾" (14.5 cm).

Number of warp ends: 45 working ends (78 actual ends).

EPI: 8.

PPI: 8.

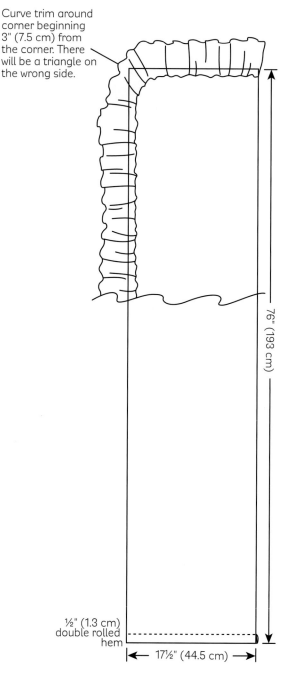

Curve trim around corner beginning 3" (7.5 cm) from the corner. There will be a triangle on the wrong side.

76" (193 cm)

½" (1.3 cm) double rolled hem

17½" (44.5 cm)

Warp color order for Ruffle:

		11x		
Autumn Flame		6*		66*
Cypress	1		1	12
			Total	78

Note: Autumn Flame is used doubled (66 actual ends but 33 working ends).

WEAVING

Weave with Merino Silk Fine Cayenne until the piece is 240" (610 cm) or until you can't weave any more. This is a long warp to accommodate on a rigid-heddle loom. We wove this on the Cricket loom that has a lot of warp and fabric storage. If beam capacity is a concern, you may want to weave this fabric in two parts.

FABRIC FINISHING (FOR BOTH FABRICS)

Handwash both pieces in hot, soapy water; lay flat to dry.

ASSEMBLY

Secure the ends with machine zigzag stitching.

Body

Cut off excess warp ends. Create a ½" (1.3 cm) double rolled hem on both ends of the cloth. Steam-press.

Making the ruffle

Pull the second and third Cypress threads along one selvedge to ruffle cloth (see page 19 for how to pull threads). Pulling from both ends of the fabric will be easiest. Once you've pulled as much as you can from one side, begin pulling from the other. The fabric will have concentrated areas of bunching that you will then even out over the length of the ruffle by smoothing with your hand. Once enough gathering is achieved to fit the length of one side of the shawl plus both ends, tie off pulled yarns to secure them. To do this, tie the two pulled threads at each end together with a square knot and trim off the excess yarn. Finish one end (you'll do the other end later) of the ruffle with a ½" (1.3 cm) double rolled hem. Leave one end unhemmed in case you need to adjust the length.

Attaching the ruffle

Lay the ruffle along three sides, pinning it in place between the second and third Cypress yarns (the pulled warp threads), overlapping the body of the cloth by ½" (1.3 cm). At the corners, create a curve, beginning 3" (7.5 cm) from the corner, leaving a triangle of cloth on the back.

If your ruffle doesn't match the other end exactly, adjust it for a perfect fit and repin. Machine stitch the ruffle on the right side ⅜" (1 cm) from the edge of the fabric. Sew slowly and help move lumpy areas under the presser foot to ease the ruffle through. When there is about 5" (12.5 cm) of ruffle left to attach, zigzag stitch and hem the other end of the ruffle so that the end of the ruffle will match the end of the ground cloth exactly. Stitch remainder of ruffle to body of cloth.

Other fabric ideas

▶ One of the things that makes this fabric so appealing is its drape. When substituting yarns, choose ones that will flow beautifully. Blending a plied bamboo yarn and a Soysilk ribbon, alternating them in the warp, would give a similar result. You could choose to alternate them in the weft or just use a single weft for faster weaving.

▶ For a study in contrast, weave up a spaced and felted fabric and trim with a narrow, shiny woven rayon ruffle.

Alternate styles

▶ Instead of a woven ruffle, create a scalloped edge with a narrow knitted or crocheted trim.

▶ Give this piece a casual look by using a rough tweed yarn for warp and weft. Weave in an oversized plaid for the body of the shawl and trim with a narrow pinstriped ruffle along the inside edge. Leave the fringe at the ends of the main fabric and add a few pom-poms to the edge—just for fun.

▶ Wrap this piece loosely around the neck, hanging down in front with the ruffle on the inside (see right).

Two warps are required for this accessory, perfect for the theater or a special celebratory night on the town. The trim fabric, a long narrow piece, is softly gathered by pulling a warp thread along the edge of one side of the strip. It is then machine stitched to all four sides of the shawl body.

STARRY, STARRY NIGHT SHAWL

Designed and woven by *Sara Goldenberg*

This sparkly creation turns an ordinary shawl into a stunning and festive wrap. The same yarn is used for warp and weft for the body of the shawl and woven in a mock waffle weave. The variegated yarn with subtle color changes and golden accents is brought to life by the longer floats of the weave structure. This is contrasted with a plain-weave trim fabric woven in a different yarn in shades of purple, dark blue, and green.

Body of Shawl

Size: one size fits most.

Finished dimensions: 15½" (39.5 cm) wide × 62" (157.5 cm) long.

Equipment: loom with 15" (38 cm) weaving width, 10-dent reed, 2 shuttles, sewing machine.

Warp yarn: *Interlacements Soya Shaft* (100% Soysilk 2-ply at 3,600 yd/lb [3,291 m/453 g], 405 yd/1.8 oz [370 m/51 g] per skein) in Forest Floor, 255 yd (233 m) or 1 skein needed. *Interlacements Irish Jig* (40% flax/31% cotton/29% rayon with metallic thread at 1,200 yd/lb [1,097 m/453 g], 600 yd/8 oz [549 m/227 g] per skein) in Oceans, 80 yd (73 m) or 1 skein needed. *Skacel Fil Royal* (100% baby alpaca at 3,017 yd/lb [2,758 m/453 g], 660 yd/3.5 oz [604 m/100 g] per skein) in color 3515, Blue Spruce, 255 yd (233 m) or 1 skein needed.

Note: Soya and Fil Royal are used together as one yarn.

Weft: *Interlacements Soya* (100% Soysilk 2-ply at 3,600 yd/lb [3,291 m/453 g], 405 yd/1.8 oz [370 m/51 g] per skein) in Blue Green, 215 yd (197 m) or 1 skein needed. *Same Fil Royal* as used for warp, 215 yd (197 m) needed. *Same Interlacements Irish Jig* as used for warp, 55 yd (50 m) needed.

Note: Use the Soya and Fil Royal together as one yarn.

Weave structure: mock waffle weave.

Warp length: 2½ yd (2.2 m), which includes take-up and 24" (61 cm) loom waste. If weaving on a shaft loom, allow 36" (91.5 cm) for loom waste and increase warp yarn yardage by one third.

Warp width: Just over 13" (33 cm).

Number of warp ends: 133 working ends (234 actual ends).

EPI: 10.

PPI: 9.

PICK-UP PATTERN FOR MOCK WAFFLE WEAVE (FOR HOW TO USE A PICK-UP STICK, SEE PAGE 17)

Pick-up stick pattern:
*2 up, 2 down; repeat from *.

Step 1: Up.

Step 2: Pick-up stick (Irish Jig).

Step 3: Up.

Step 4: Pick-up stick (Irish Jig).

Step 5: Up.

Step 6: Down.

Step 7: Up and pick-up stick.

Step 8: Down.

Step 9: Up and pick-up stick.

Step 10: Down.

Step 11: Steps 1–10 for pattern. To balance at the end of the weaving, end with Steps 1–5.

DRAFT FOR STARRY, STARRY NIGHT

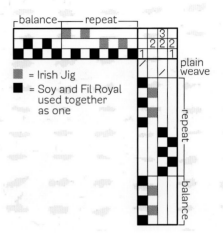

= Irish Jig

= Soy and Fil Royal used together as one

Warp color order:

	Repeat 16 x			end	
S & FR*	10**		2	10	202*
Irish Jig		1		1	32
			Total warp ends		234***

Note: Irish Jig will be used in the slots only.

*S = Soya and FR = Fil Royal These yarns are used together as one. 202 actual ends (101 of Soya and 101 of Fil Royal).
***Actual ends (133 working ends).

**start in a hole

WEAVING

Step 1: Weave 1½" (3.8 cm) of plain weave for the rolled hem edge.

Step 2: Weave for 61" (155 cm) in mock waffle weave.

Step 3: Weave 1½" (3.8 cm) of plain weave for rolled hem edge.

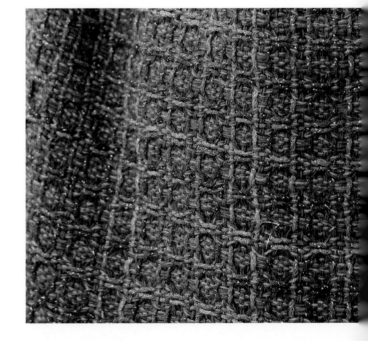

Ruffle

Finished dimensions: 2½" × 8¼ yd (6.5 × 7.5 m).

Warp yarn: *Interlacements Zig Zag* (98% rayon/2% nylon at 1,450 yd/lb [1,326 m/453 g], 725 yd/8 oz [663 m/227 g] per skein) in Submarine, 135 yd (123 m) or 1 skein needed. Same Irish Jig as used in the first warp, 135 yd (123 m) needed.

Weft yarn: same Zig Zag as used for the warp, 267 yd (244 m) needed.

Weave structure: plain weave.

Warp length: 9 yd (8.2 m), which includes take-up and 24" (61 cm) loom waste. If weaving on a shaft loom, allow 36" (91.5 cm) for loom waste and increase warp yarn yardage by a third.

Note: If your loom will not accommodate a 9 yd (8.2 m) warp length, you can weave the ruffle trim in two pieces and join them after weaving.

Warp width: 3" (7.5 cm).

Number of warp ends: 30, 15 of Zig Zag and 15 of Irish Jig.

Warp color order: alternate Zig Zag and Irish Jig, threading the Irish Jig in the slots.

EPI: 10.

PPI: 9.

WEAVING

Use Zig Zag and weave plain weave until the end of the warp.

FABRIC FINISHING (FOR BOTH FABRICS)

Secure the ends with overhand knots and handwash in hot, soapy water. Let the fabrics sit for 3–5 minutes before rinsing. Lay flat to dry. While still slightly damp, put the fabrics in the dryer on delicate for about 5 minutes to full it a little more. Watch closely!

ASSEMBLY

Step 1: Prepare the body of the shawl. Using the 1½" (3.8 cm) of plain weave on either end, create a double rolled hem. Press, pin, and stitch into place by hand or on the sewing machine. This piece will measure about 60" (152.5 cm) long.

Step 2: Ruffle the trim by pulling the second thread in from one selvedge edge (the Irish Jig pulls smoothly). Pull from both ends of fabric and smooth out to get an even ruffle all the way around.

Step 3: Pin the ruffle in place around all 4 edges, overlapping the edge of the body fabric about ½" (1.3 cm). Adjust as needed so that the ruffle is even around all of the edges. When you are certain you have the right amount of pull in your warp to make

the ruffle lie evenly all the way around, fold over one edge of ruffle with a ½" (1.3 cm) single-fold hem. Steam-press and stitch.

Note: To eliminate bulk where the ends of the ruffle connect, be sure that it is the appropriate length all the way around. This may take readjusting until you have it right.

Step 4: Stitch the ruffle to the body of the shawl all the way around on the sewing machine, stopping 4" (10 cm) from the end to double-check the point at which you need to hem the other end. You may need to cut off excess or let a little bit of length out of the ruffle to make it right. Fold the end in the opposite direction so that the folded edges of the ruffle overlap. Once you know the length is correct, sew a single-fold hem on the other end. Secure the last 4" (10 cm) of the ruffle to the base of the shawl. Stitch overlapped ends of the ruffle together.

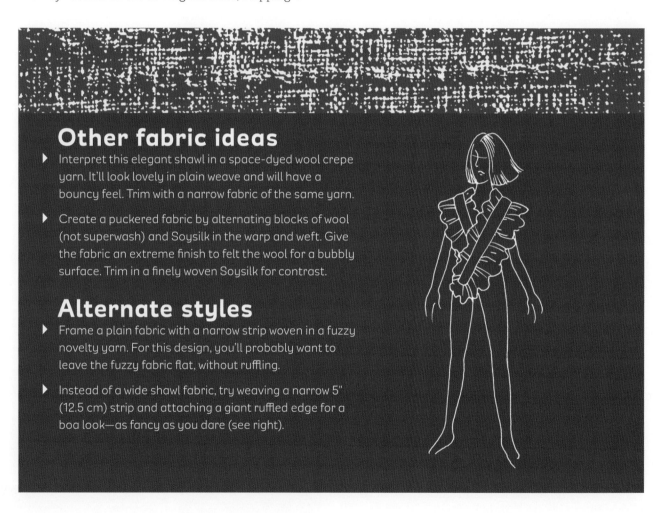

Other fabric ideas

▶ Interpret this elegant shawl in a space-dyed wool crepe yarn. It'll look lovely in plain weave and will have a bouncy feel. Trim with a narrow fabric of the same yarn.

▶ Create a puckered fabric by alternating blocks of wool (not superwash) and Soysilk in the warp and weft. Give the fabric an extreme finish to felt the wool for a bubbly surface. Trim in a finely woven Soysilk for contrast.

Alternate styles

▶ Frame a plain fabric with a narrow strip woven in a fuzzy novelty yarn. For this design, you'll probably want to leave the fuzzy fabric flat, without ruffling.

▶ Instead of a wide shawl fabric, try weaving a narrow 5" (12.5 cm) strip and attaching a giant ruffled edge for a boa look—as fancy as you dare (see right).

Two rectangles are joined to make this a topper that could be dressed up over a long neutral dress or dressed down over a T-shirt and jeans. Either way, it's easy to make and lovely to wear. A fine alpaca yarn is used for the warp and is crossed with a mohair/silk blend for a fabric that is featherweight light, yet warm.

GREEN-GRAY TOPPER

Designed by *Jane Patrick and Sara Goldenberg*; woven and sewn by *Sara Goldenberg*

The stripes are created by skipping dents in the reed. The fabric is then turned in the garment for horizontal stripes. A separate, narrow warp was woven for the joining tabs at the shoulders and sides. These offer detailing to the garment and provide stability at stress points.

Body

Garment size: medium.

Finished dimensions: 29½" (75 cm) wide × 18" (45.5 cm) deep.

Equipment: loom with 20" (51 cm) weaving width, 12-dent reed, shuttle, tapestry needle, sewing thread and needle, sewing machine.

Warp yarn: *Alpaca with a Twist Fino* (70% baby alpaca/30% silk at 3,972 yd/lb [3,632 m/453 g], 875 yd/3.52 oz [800 m/100 g] per skein) in color 0098, Silver Belle, 530 yd (485 m) or 1 skein needed for garment and tabs.

Weft yarn: *Trendsetter Kid Seta* (70% mohair/30% silk at 405 yd/lb [370 m/453 g] 230 yd/9.13 oz [210 m/259 g] per ball) in color #368, Olive, 325 yd (297 m) or 2 balls needed for garment and tabs.

Weave structure: plain weave with spaced warps.

Warp length: 2⅝ yd (2.5 m), which includes take-up and 24" (61 cm) loom waste. If weaving on a shaft loom, allow 36" (91.5 cm) for loom waste and increase warp yarn yardage by a third.

Warp width: 19.5" (49.5 cm).

Total warp ends: 192.

EPI: 12.

PPI: 7.

Warping plan:

Fino	24		30		24		18		18		24		30		24
Empty		6		6		6		6		6		6		6	

Note: There are 234 spaces either filled with a thread or left empty.

WEAVING

At the beginning and end of the weaving, weave about 2" (5 cm) with another yarn. This will help maintain the warp spacing. This is waste yarn and will be removed later. Weave in plain weave using mohair. Measure without tension until fabric measures 68" (172.5 cm).

If you do not want to secure the edges on the sewing machine after weaving, hemstitch (see page 9 for how to hemstitch) at both ends of each panel. If hemstitching, end first panel at 34" (86.5 cm) and hemstitch. Weave a 1" (2.5 cm) spacer and hemstitch again at the beginning of the next panel.

FABRIC FINISHING

Securely roll the fabric up in a thin towel, tie the bundle with wool yarn (the wool will shrink in the finishing process and keep the roll tight), and place it a pillowcase. Wash in the washing machine in hot water on regular cycle with mild soap. Check after 5 minutes and reverse orientation of the fabric in towel so that the inside of the roll is now closest to outside. Full for 5 more minutes. This will help even out the fulling, as the outside felts quicker than the inside (it is harder for the soap and agitation to penetrate to the core of the roll). If the fabric is not fulled enough, repeat for another 2–5 minutes, watching closely.

Tabs

Warp and weft yarns: use the same Fino for warp and mohair/silk for weft.

Weave structure: plain weave.

Warp length: 2 yd (1.8 m), which includes take-up and 24" (61 cm) loom waste. If weaving on a shaft loom, allow 36" (91.5 cm) for loom waste and increase warp yarn yardage by a third.

Warp width: ¾" (2 cm).

Number of warp ends: 9.

EPI: 12.

PPI: 7.

WEAVING

Because this is a narrow warp, there will be a tendency for the weft to pack in tightly. Use a light beat. You will need 12 tabs in all (at each attachment point there are 2 tabs, one on the inside and one on the outside).

Prepare the tabs: Prepare 12 tabs, each 4" (10 cm) long. Zigzag stitch across on either side of the cutting lines and cut apart (see illustration).

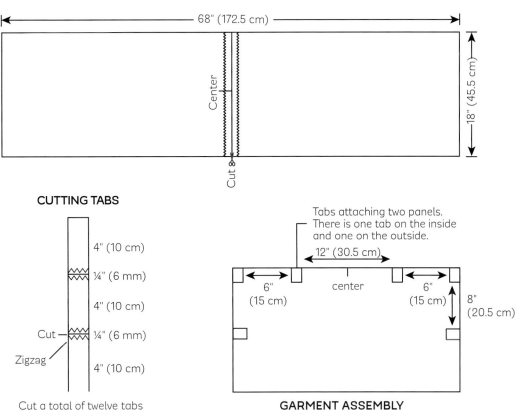

68" (172.5 cm)

Center

Cut

18" (45.5 cm)

CUTTING TABS

4" (10 cm)

¼" (6 mm)

4" (10 cm)

Cut — ¼" (6 mm)

Zigzag

4" (10 cm)

Cut a total of twelve tabs

Tabs attaching two panels. There is one tab on the inside and one on the outside.

12" (30.5 cm)

6" (15 cm)

center

6" (15 cm)

8" (20.5 cm)

GARMENT ASSEMBLY

ASSEMBLY

Divide the garment fabric in half and mark ¼" (6 mm) on either side of the cutting centerline. Using a medium-length stitch, zigzag and then straight stitch on either side of centerline and cut fabric apart, making two pieces. The straight stitch is helpful to stabilize the gaps in the warp.

Hem the ends of both panels by stitching a ¼" (6 mm) double rolled hem by hand or with the sewing machine.

Place the 2 hemmed panels one on top of the other, wrong sides together. Find the center along one of the long edges and mark with a pin. Measure out 6" (15 cm) on either side for a 12" (30.5 cm) neck hole.

To secure the panels together, machine or handsew the tabs on the front and back at the points shown on page 43. There will be two tabs at each point, one on the right side and one on the wrong side. Half of each tab will be on one panel and half on the other. Pin in place. Fold the raw edges under ¼" (6 mm) and handstitch or sew by machine to secure.

Place tabs in these places (see illustration on page 43):

▸ At 6" (15 cm) mark from either side of center (for neck hole)

▸ At each side of the shoulder (at each end of the fabric edge)

▸ Along each side, 8" (20.5 cm) from the top shoulder edge

Other fabric ideas

▶ This garment should be light. If it is too heavy, it will look like a blanket. Textural accents, whether they be yarn- or weave-centric, will go a long way to creating a smashing accessory.

▶ For a different weave structure, try paired warp floats (these will appear as horizontal stripes in the top) or stacked Brooks bouquet (which will also give a horizontal line when turned during construction).

▶ For yarn ideas, you could use the same warping pattern as our original but substitute a handpainted sock yarn in the warp and insert a wool loop yarn in the areas left unthreaded in the reed. This idea would lend itself to a lofty novelty yarn or a combination of them.

Alternate styles

▶ Go short and add a beaded fringe for a casual look. Use contrasting material for tabs such as Ultrasuede or even a contrasting ribbon (see top, right).

▶ Instead of turning the fabric in the construction, use the warp vertically in the garment. Warp stripes will appear as slimming verticals in the piece. Stitch the shoulders together and slightly taper the sides, leaving vents at the bottom edge to ease the fit (see bottom, right).

▶ Take this idea to a whole other dimension by weaving 2 very large panels and stitching all of the seams instead of using tabs. Belt or gather at the waistband.

Alternating blocks of warp floats allow the outlining weft yarn to curve, creating sparkling lozenges in a field of gray. Tencel is a wonderful yarn choice for a garment, because it has a beautiful sheen and drape.

HONEYCOMB BOATNECK TOP

Designed by *Jane Patrick and Sara Goldenberg*; woven by *David Pipinich*

We'd say that this garment is about as simple as it gets, construction-wise. Two rectangles are woven and sewn together. We added a little shaping at the armholes and neckline for a finished look. Since the fabric is turned sideways in the construction, horizontal weft stripes become vertical in the garment. If you want horizontal stripes in your garment, design them in the warp.

Garment size: medium.

Finished dimensions: 29½" wide × 23" deep (75 × 58.5 cm).

Equipment: loom with 25" (63. 5 cm) weaving width, 3 shuttles, sewing machine. If weaving on a rigid-heddle loom, you'll need 2 pick-up sticks and two 12-dent rigid-heddle reeds.

Warp yarn: *8/2 Tencel from WEBS* (3,360 yd/lb [3,072 m/453 g], available on 1 lb [453 g] cones) in Shale, 1,800 yd (1,646 m) or 1 cone needed for warp and weft.

Weft yarn: Same *8/2 Tencel* used for warp, used doubled; 1,300 yd (1,189 m) needed. *Crystal Olympus from EmmaCreations* (100% polyester at 3,163 yd/lb [2,892 m/453 g], 74 yd/.88 oz [160 m/25 g] per ball) color #7, 78 yd (71 m) or 1 ball

needed. *Adele from Tahki-Stacy Charles Inc.* (43% viscose/28% polyester/20% kid mohair/9% polyamide, 1,545 yd/lb [1,415 m/453 g], 169 yd/1.75 oz [155 m/50 g] per ball) in color #24, Gold, 120 yd (110 m) or 1 ball needed.

Weave structure: honeycomb (see box on page 51).

Warp length: 3 yd (2.75 m), which includes take-up and

24" (61 cm) loom waste. If weaving on a shaft loom, allow 36" [91.5 cm] for loom waste and increase warp yarn yardage by a third.

Warp width: 25" (63.5 cm).

Number of warp ends: 600.

EPI: 24.

PPI: 13–14.

Note: Tencel is used doubled in the weft.

PICK-UP PATTERN FOR HONEYCOMB

Pick-up stick pattern A:
*5 up, 5 down; repeat from *.

Pick-up stick pattern B:
*5 down, 5 up; repeat from *.

WEAVE BLOCK A
(PICK-UP STICK PATTERN A)

Step 1: Up, accent yarn (Adele).

Step 2: Down, accent yarn (Adele).

Step 3: Up and pick-up stick (Tencel or Crystal).

Step 4: Down (Tencel or Crystal).

Step 5: Up and pick-up stick (Tencel or Crystal).

Step 6: Down (Tencel or Crystal).

Step 7: Up and pick-up stick (Tencel or Crystal).

Step 8: Down (Tencel or Crystal).

WEAVE BLOCK B
(PICK-UP STICK PATTERN B)

Step 9: Insert pick-up stick B and repeat Steps 1–8.

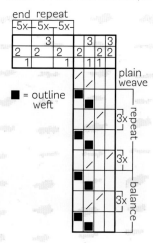

DRAFT FOR HONEYCOMB

WEAVING

Weave each panel for 35" (89 cm). Use Tencel doubled, interspersing cells of Crystal Olympus (replacing the Tencel background yarn) for highlights. Sparkly Adele outlines all of the cells. Use an even beat and advance your warp often.

Side 1 (use either side for the front or back): Weave 1" (2.5 cm) of plain weave for hem. Alternating Block A and Block B for the entire fabric, weave the yarns as follows: 6 blocks (alternate Block A and Block B 3 times for a total of 6 blocks) Tencel, 2 blocks Crystal, 8 blocks Tencel, 1 block Crystal, 3 blocks Tencel, 1 block Crystal, 2 blocks Tencel, 1 block Crystal, 8 blocks Tencel, 1 block Crystal, 8 blocks Tencel, 2 blocks Crystal, 3 blocks Tencel.

Side 2: Weave 2" (5 cm) of plain weave and then begin pattern for second side: 7 blocks Tencel, 1 block Crystal, 7 blocks Tencel, 1 block Crystal, 2 blocks Tencel, 1 block Crystal, 3 blocks Tencel, 2 blocks Crystal, 6 blocks Tencel, 1 block Crystal, 1 block Tencel, 1 block Crystal, 8 blocks Tencel, 2 blocks Crystal, 3 blocks Tencel. End with 1" (2.5 cm) of plain weave for hem.

Alternately, you could make up your own pattern.

FABRIC FINISHING

Handwash in warm, soapy water. Lay flat to dry.

ASSEMBLY

If machine stitching, zigzag stitch 2 rows in the center of the plain weave between the front and back panels. Leave about ¼" (6 mm) of space between rows and then cut the panels apart. Zigzag outer edges of fabric and cut off fringe.

Step 1: Create ½" (1.3 cm) double rolled hem on edges on both sides of each panel. Steam-press and pin hems, then stitch by hand or on the sewing machine.

Step 2: With right sides together, find the center of both panels. Measure out from the center 6" (15 cm) on either side. This 12" (30.5 cm) area will be your neck opening. Pin from neck-hole edges to end of fabric. Hand baste and then sew with a ⅝" (1.5 cm) seam allowance from the outside edge in.

Step 3: Steam-press down the ⅝" (1.5 cm) amount of fabric that would have been part of the seam if there were no neck hole. Hand tack in place along the neckline from the wrong side of the garment across both sides of the neck hole.

Step 4: Create the armhole openings. Working with the garment wrong sides together, measure down 10" (25.5 cm) from the shoulder seam. Pin the two sides together. Handstitch these seams with a butt join (the edges of the rolled hems butting up against each other instead of overlapping). This reduces bulk.

BUTT JOIN

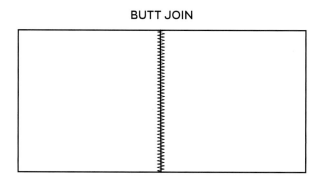

BOATNECK LAYOUT

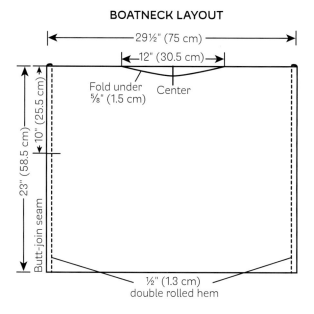

29½" (75 cm)

12" (30.5 cm)

Fold under ⅝" (1.5 cm) Center

10" (25.5 cm)

23" (58.5 cm)

Butt-join seam

½" (1.3 cm) double rolled hem

VARIATION

Designed and woven by Sara Goldenberg
For this summery variation, we used Tencel in pale pink for the warp and gold, coral, and mauve for the weft, outlining them with a deep blue fingering-weight wool yarn. The warp, sett at 20 ends per inch, and the weft are Tencel. We altered the weaving pattern for wavy lozenges on the sides and alternated small and large cells in the center. The asymmetrical pattern lends a lighthearted look.

Other fabric ideas

▶ For a different patterned look, try an all plain-weave ground with a sprinkling of honeycomb accents, regularly spaced or at random.

▶ A simple warp stripe can be turned in the garment for horizontal stripes. For ideas, check tops or dresses in your closet for patterns you already like and interpret these in your handwoven fabric.

Alternate styles

▶ Use the same construction with broad warp stripes for horizontal stripes in the garment.

▶ Cut a V-neck in the front of one panel and trim with a narrow woven or knitted trim (see right).

▶ Give this top a tunic look by weaving longer lengths of fabric and using them vertically instead of horizontally. Fringy edges lend a casual look.

HONEYCOMB

Weaving is a grid in which yarns are held in place by the crossing of warp and weft. However, the yarns will escape the grid if allowed the space in the woven web to do so. Almost magical, a honeycomb weave is one in which yarns are allowed space to escape the woven grid to create wavy lines in the cloth. It is a phenomenon called deflection in which yarns are allowed to move because they have the space to do so.

There are many kinds of honeycomb. Generally, on a rigid-heddle loom, you have two blocks to play with. The wavy lines you see in the weft are actually created by groups of warp threads, or blocks. As one block is woven, warp floats are created that create room for the weft to undulate. When the other block is woven, the weft moves in the opposite direction. The deeper the block, the bigger the curve. This is limited only by the practicality of the warp float lengths.

For this honeycomb top, for example, the pick-up pattern for block A is 5 up, 5 down, and the pattern for block B is 5 down, 5 up. You can see that these blocks are opposites of each other. The curving weft takes place when 2 picks of plain weave in a contrasting yarn are woven between blocks.

▲ Picking block A.

▲ Weaving block A.

▲ Weaving 2 rows of plain weave between blocks.

▲ Picking block B.

Combine your weaving and knitting skills for this fashionable garment. The chainette yarn "makes" this cozy garment, creating a sweater you'll return to again and again for comfort and style. Two rectangles are joined at the shoulders and sides; a knitted collar and sleeves add shape.

COWL-NECK SWEATER

Designed and woven by *Sara Goldenberg*

The bouncy chainette yarn used for the bulk of this piece gives it a knitted look. We threaded this yarn in the warp and then alternated it with a thinner yarn in a contrasting color in the weft. The knitted cowl collar and the short knitted sleeves are the final accents that transform two rectangles into a sweater.

Garment size: small/medium.

Finished dimensions: 28" (71 cm) wide (across the shoulder to knit sleeves) and 20" (51 cm) deep (shoulder to bottom). The cowl measures 5" (12.5 cm) deep, folded; sleeves measure 3½" (9 cm) long.

Equipment: loom with 25" (63.5 cm) weaving width, 5-dent reed, 2 shuttles, sewing machine (optional), size J or K crochet hook, 24" (61 cm) size 11 circular knitting needle and 16" (40.5 cm) size 10½ circular knitting needle.

Gauge: 13 stitches and 23 rows in 4" (10 cm).

Warp yarn: *Berroco Voyage* (93% alpaca/7% polyester at 1,143 yd/lb [1,045 m/453 g], 125 yd /1.75 oz [114 m/50 g] per skein) in color #4015, Coastline, 375 yd (343 m) or 3 skeins needed.

Weft yarn: same *Berroco Voyage* yarn used for warp, 250 yd (229 m) or 2 skeins needed; *Berroco Seduce* (47% rayon/25% viscose/17% linen/11% silk at 1,135 yd/lb [1,038 m/453 g], 100 yd/1.41 oz [92 m/40 g] per skein) in color #4437, 250 yd (229 m) or 3 skeins needed.

Yarn for knitted trim: same Voyage yarn as above, 375 yd (343 m) or 3 skeins needed.

Weave structure: plain weave.

Warp length: 3 yd (2.75 m), which includes take-up and 24" (61 cm) loom waste. If weaving on a shaft loom, allow 36" (91.5 cm) for loom waste and increase warp yarn yardage by a third.

Warp width: 25" (63.5 cm).

Number of warp ends: 125.

EPI: 5.

PPI: 8.

WEAVING

Hemstitch the beginning and end of the weaving using 2 picks of plain weave, in Voyage, and bundles of 2 warp threads. Because the Voyage yarn is springy and thick, hemstitching is recommended instead of a rolled hem in this design. *Note: We experienced 20% take-up in the warp and 16% draw-in in the weft. You can minimize this by using minimal tension and laying the weft into the shed with little tension.*

Weave in plain weave alternating picks of Voyage and Seduce. (See page 10 for information about interlocking wefts when using two shuttles.) The Voyage yarn has a lot of stretch; it is therefore prudent to lay it into the shed rather than pulling it. Allowing the yarn to relax while weaving will help to minimize draw-in.

The fabric will be turned for construction. This means that the selvedges will be exposed at the bottom edge of the sweater, so you'll want to take care to interlock weft picks when the Seduce and Voyage are on the same side of the warp. To accurately gauge your fabric length, measure off-tension as you go until you've woven 35" (89 cm) for the first panel. Hemstitch. Weave 3"–4" (7.5–10 cm) with scrap yarn in similar size between the first and second panels. Hemstitch and weave the second panel just like the first one. End with hemstitching.

FABRIC FINISHING

Remove the fabric from the loom and handwash lightly in warm, soapy water. Lay flat to dry.

ASSEMBLY

Step 1: Cut the panels apart, trim fringe to about ½" (1.3 cm) on either side of both panels. (Alternately, you can run the ends of the fabric through the sewing machine using a long stitch for added security.) Stack the panels on top of one another.

Step 2: Find the center point of the panels and mark with a pin.

Step 3: Measure out 5½" (13.5 cm) on either side of the center, marking these two points with pins as well. This will yield an 11" wide (28 cm) neck-hole opening.

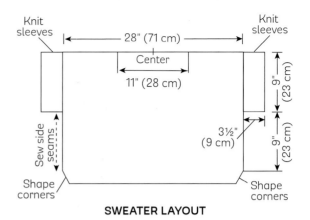

SWEATER LAYOUT

Step 4: After marking the neck-hole opening, handsew the top edges of the panels together on either side of the neck hole, using a single strand of Voyage yarn. This will create a seam along the shoulders.

Use a butt-joined overcast seam for the shoulder seam (see page 49).

KNITTING THE COWL

For how to pick up stitches, see page 20.

Step 1: Leaving a tail to sew in later, use a crochet hook and Voyage yarn to pick up 55 stitches evenly around the neck hole, placing them on 24" (61 cm) size 11 circular needle.

Step 2: Move stitches from crochet hook to knitting needle every 5 stitches. Be sure to pick up an odd number of stitches.

Step 3: Join yarn and knit with the wrong side facing out (when folded down for wearing it will be right side out).

Step 4: Knit 10 rows.

Step 5: *Increase row.* Starting with a M1 (make 1), M1 every fifth stitch (increase of 11). You'll have a total of 66 stitches. The neck has a sequence of increases so that the cowl has a subtle flare.

Step 6: Knit 4 rows.

Step 7: *Increase row.* M1 every 5th stitch (increase of 13). You'll have a total of 79 stitches.

Step 8: Knit 4 rows.

Step 9: *Increase row.* Starting with a M1, M1 every fifth stitch (increase of 16). You'll have a total of 95 stitches.

Step 10: Knit 20 rows.

Step 11: Switch to seed stitch (working with odd number of stitches) for 9 rows. *Row 1:* k1 p1; *Row 2:* p1, k1. Repeat from * 4 times and end with k1, p2.

Step 12: Cast off in seed stitch.

KNITTING THE SLEEVES

Step 1: Leaving a long tail to sew in later, use a crochet hook to pull the Voyage yarn up from the wrong side of the fabric every 2 warp threads. Pull the yarn through on top of the first pick of Seduce and after the hemstitched row. You should have 67 stitches.

Step 2: Join yarn and knit on 16" (40.5 cm) size 10½ circular needle in stockinette stitch for 17 rows (knit every round).

Step 3: Knit 3 rows of seed stitch and cast off in seed stitch.

Step 4: Repeat Steps 1–3 for other sleeve.

Finish assembly by sewing up side seams with a butt join using Voyage yarn from the bottom of armhole until 2" (5 cm) above the bottom edge of the piece. This creates a little vent at the bottom of the sweater. Fold vent under, tapering from 0" at the top of the vent to ¾" (2 cm) at the bottom edge. Handstitch in place.

Other fabric ideas

- You'll want a fabric that is soft and drapable. This is one of the reasons we love chainette yarn: it has loft and bulk but is springy and soft. Many yarn companies are offering this type of yarn, and we encourage you to try it out. A mohair blend alternated in warp and weft with alpaca plied yarn will be a lovely choice for a fabric that is light and fuzzy.

- For this project, we used a solid warp and alternated two different yarns in the weft. We then turned the fabric for vertical stripes. Placing the stripes in the warp will produce horizontal lines, a plus in that only one shuttle is required for weaving.

- A subtle plaid in a soft bouclé might be worth sampling as well.

Alternate styles

You can do so much with two rectangles. Here are some other design ideas to play around with:

- Weave long, narrower panels for a hip-length sweater vest, cut a V-neck, and accent the armholes and neckline with knitted or crocheted trim (see right).

- Weave narrower panels for a short, cropped top. Place stripes in the warp and add a knitted turtleneck trim.

- Weave 2 panels and cut one down the center for a cardigan-style top. A curved neckline will be attractive worn over a turtleneck sweater. Add a simple blanket-stitch edging for a finishing touch.

We thought that tabards were a thing of the past—like the woolly 1970s past—but when we saw a hip and stylish one in the Nordstrom catalog, we decided it was time to bring this old favorite back, with a twist. The update is a perky, textured fabric that is light and lofty.

TABARD

Designed by *Jane Patrick and Sara Goldenberg*; woven by *Sara Goldenberg*

This is easy: weave two rectangles and a narrow band for the straps and side attachments, give the fabrics a vigorous washing, and simply attach the straps. Voila! Your tabard is ready to wear.

To create the fabric, we used one wool yarn that would felt and a superwash wool that would not. We used wool for the weft, except at the bottom edges where we used the superwash for a bubble border. There's something else, too: to produce the layer-on-layer effect, we used a weft float pattern to create horizontal lines over the variegated stripes. Behind the latticelike floats, lines of variegated sock yarn give a weave-on-weave appearance.

Main Fabric

Garment size: medium.

Finished dimensions: 34" (86.5 cm) from top of straps to bottom, 19" (48.5 cm) wide from the center of straps on either side of each panel.

Equipment: loom with at least 25" (63.5 cm) weaving width, 5-dent reed, 2 shuttles, washing machine, sewing machine.

Warp yarn (for both warps): *Brown Sheep Nature Spun*, sportweight (100% wool at 2,355 yd/lb [2,154 m/453 g], 184 yd/1.75 oz [168 m/50 g] per ball) in color N46 Red Fox, 300 yd (275 m) or 2 balls needed.

Warp yarn (for main fabric only): *Brown Sheep Wildfoote* sock yarn (75% washable wool/25% nylon at 1,966 yd/lb [1,825 m/kg], 215 yd/1.75 oz [197 m/50 g] per skein) in color #SY150, Acappella, 208 yd (190 m) needed or 1 ball; and color #SY600, Symphony, 156 yd (143 m) or 1 ball needed. *Note: Both Wildfoote yarns are used doubled.*

Weft yarn (for both warps): *Brown Sheep Nature Spun*, sportweight (100% wool at 2,355 yd/lb [2154 m/453 g], 184 yd/1.75 oz [168 m/50 g] per ball) in color #145 Salmon, 352 yd (322 m) or 2 balls needed.

Weft yarn (for main fabric only): *Brown Sheep Wildfoote*, sock yarn (75% washable wool/25% nylon at 1,966 yd/lb [1,798 m/kg], 215 yd/1.75 oz [197 m/50 g] per skein) in color #SY600, Symphony, 35 yd (32 m) or 1 ball needed. *Note: Wildfoote is used doubled.*

Weave structure: plain weave with weft float patterning.

Warp length: 3¼ yd (3 m) which includes take-up and 24" (61 cm) loom waste. If weaving on a shaft loom, allow 36" (91.5 cm) for loom waste and increase warp yarn yardage by a third.

Warp width: 25" (63.5 cm).

Number of warp ends: 124 working ends (180 actual ends).

EPI: 5.

PPI: 6.

PICK-UP STICK PATTERN: 5 UP, *4 DOWN, 4 UP; REPEAT FROM * 6 TIMES. END WITH 4 DOWN AND 5 UP.

Step 1: Up.

Step 2: Pick-up stick.

Step 3: Up.

Step 4: Pick-up stick.

Step 5: Up.

Step 6: Down.

Repeat Steps 1–6 for pattern.

DRAFT FOR MAIN FABRIC

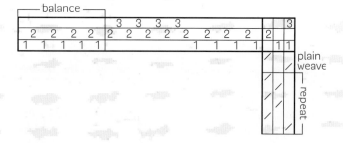

Warp color order:

		Repeat 3 times				
NS	10		8		8	10	68
WA*		16			16		64*
WS*			16				48*
			Total number of warp ends				180^^

NS = Nature Spun; WA = Wildfoote in Acappella, *used doubled. WS = Wildfoote in Symphony, *used doubled. Note: WA = 64 actual ends and 32 working ends; WS = 48 actual ends and 24 working ends.

^^180 actual ends and 124 working ends.

WEAVING

Because this fabric is going to be felted, you'll want to weave with a loose beat at 6 picks per inch. Be careful to not overbeat and measure often.

Step 1: Weave hem with Nature Spun in Salmon for 2¼" (5.5 cm).

Step 2: Weave the bottom border—5 picks Wildfoote, 3 picks Nature Spun, 5 picks Wildfoote. Remember: Wildfoote is used doubled.

Step 3: Weave the body of the panel for about 75" (190.5 cm) with Nature Spun and pick-up pattern.

Step 4: Weave the border as in Step 2 and finish with 2¼" (6 cm) hem as you began.

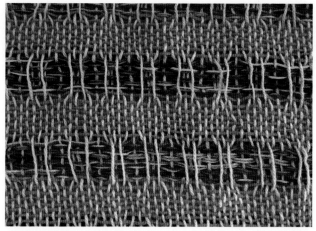

▲ Fabric before washing.

FABRIC FINISHING

Secure the ends of the weaving with overhand knots. Machine wash, regular cycle, for about 12 minutes. Use hot water and regular laundry detergent. Check often to see how the felting is coming along. Rinse in cold water once felting is complete. Lay flat to dry.

Note: If wrapping and tying up in a towel to felt the fabric, we recommend cutting the cloth in half before felting. Also, midway through the cycle, you'll want to unroll your fabric to see how it is felting. At this point, put what was on the outside of the towel on the inside so as to achieve even felting along the entire length of the fabric.

Plain-weave areas will shrink less than the float areas.

Tabs

Finished dimensions: 5½" (14 cm) wide × 48" (122 cm) long.

Warp and weft yarns: Brown Sheep Nature Spun in Red Fox is used for warp and Brown Sheep Nature Spun in Salmon is used for weft. Quantities needed are included in total yardage on page 57.

Weave structure: plain weave.

Warp length: 2¼ yd (2 m).

Warp width: 6" (15 cm).

Number of warp ends: 30.

EPI: 5.

PPI: 5.

WEAVING

Weave plain weave until the warp runs out using an even beat. Mind your selvedges, as they will show in the finished garment.

FABRIC FINISHING

Secure the ends with overhand knots. Machine wash for about 10 minutes on a regular cycle in hot water and laundry detergent. Rinse in cold water and lay flat to dry.

ASSEMBLY

Step 1: Cut 4 tabs to 7" (18 cm) each (we suggest using a rotary cutter and healing mat for crisp cuts). You don't need to zigzag stitch the ends because the felting process has stabilized the fabric.

Step 2: Cut the fringe off both ends of tabard fabric.

Step 3: At both ends of the tabard fabric, make a 1" (2.5 cm) double rolled hem along the fabric in plain weave so that the bottom edges of the cloth are the first bands of Wildfoote.

Step 4: To keep the bubbles puffy, steam-press only between them along the hem.

Step 5: Stitch hems on the sewing machine with a long stitch length just below first bubble row.

Step 6: After bottom edges are hemmed, find the center of cloth (lengthwise) and cut in half. Again, a rotary cutter and healing mat make neat work. If

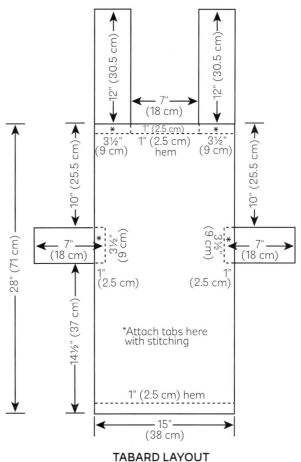

12" (30.5 cm)

7" (18 cm)

12" (30.5 cm)

1" (2.5 cm)

3½" (9 cm)

1" (2.5 cm) hem

3½" (9 cm)

10" (25.5 cm)

10" (25.5 cm)

28" (71 cm)

7" (18 cm)

3½" (9 cm)

3½" (9 cm)

7" (18 cm)

1" (2.5 cm)

1" (2.5 cm)

14½" (37 cm)

*Attach tabs here with stitching

1" (2.5 cm) hem

15" (38 cm)

TABARD LAYOUT

you find that you have more length than you want, adjust it accordingly by cutting off fabric from the nonhemmed ends.

Step 7: At the top edges, along Salmon floats, press edges under 1" (2.5 cm). Machine stitch with a long stitch length ½" (1.3 cm) from edge. Panels will measure 28" (71 cm) after 1" (2.5 cm) fold on either end.

Step 8: On the wrong side, attach the shoulder tabs two warp yarns in from the selvedges and 1" (2.5 cm) down from top edge. Pin both tabs to front panel first and then to the back panel.

Step 9: So they don't slide, hand baste the tabs into place before machine stitching. On the right side, topstitch across all of the tabs for a clean edge.

Step 10: On the wrong side of the front, attach the side tabs 10" (25.5 cm) down from top of garment. Hand baste in place with a 1" (2.5 cm) overlap, then topstitch with the sewing machine.

Step 11: Try on and adjust the side tabs for a proper fit. Stitch in place as for the front side of the tab. Hand baste and then machine stitch. For this piece, we left 4½" (11.5 cm) between the front and back panels.

Step 12: Handstitch the other side of the tabs and then topstitch.

Alternately: Depending on how snug you want the piece to fit, you can attach the back of one tab and attach the second with two snaps for easier in and out of the garment.

Other fabric ideas

▶ Using a nonwashable wool, weave a loose mock waffle-weave fabric with a contrasting yarn for the long warp and weft floats. After weaving, give the fabric a vigorous fulling. The weave structure will be obscured, leaving a textured surface.

▶ Try cotton for a crisp fabric. A variegated yarn woven in both warp and weft will create a plaidlike look. This is easy to weave with a great result.

▶ If you don't want to weave a pick-up pattern, try interpreting this idea by leaving spaces in the reed as well as spaces unwoven in the weft and then felting it all for an open, yet stable fabric. You could use the same Brown Sheep Nature Spun but not the Wildfoote, which is a superwash wool and won't felt.

Alternate styles

▶ Interpret this idea for an apron. Weave one panel in a dense cotton yarn and add long ties around the neck and waist. You could have a lot of fun with contrasting colors: an all-blue apron with red ties at the neck and yellow ones around the waist. Or think plaid or narrow vertical stripes.

▶ Weave very short panels for a cropped vest and trim with contrasting tabs (see right).

▶ Using the same basic garment construction, forgo the side tabs and belt with a soft broad belt.

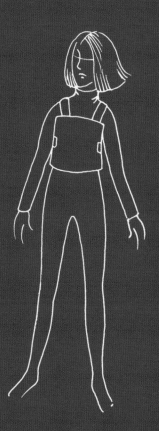

One of the joys of weaving is the excitement of discovery—and there's a lot to explore in creating this engaging top. From perfecting selvedges, to trying your hand at plaid, to shaped felting, who thought there'd be so much to learn with just one little top?

CAMISOLE

Designed and woven by *Nancy McRay*

Three separate warps are used to create this little number. Since selvedges form the bottom edge on the narrow "skirt" and the top edge of the bodice, you'll want to be mindful of weaving perfect selvedges with a nice even beat. To shape the bodice, spot felting is used along with a weft float pattern, which adds to and assists the felting process. If you can't bring yourself to make three separate warps (although, if you're new to weaving, it'd be great practice), you could weave the bodice and skirt both on the same warp, perhaps varying the weft color on one.

Garment size: medium.

Finished dimensions: for bust size 36" (91.5 cm): 18" (46 cm) across the bodice (side to side), 19" (48 cm) from top of straps to bottom of the skirt.

Equipment: loom with at least 9" (23 cm) weaving width, 12-dent reed, 2 shuttles, 2 pick-up sticks, sewing machine.

Notions: one size 3 hook and eye.

Yarn: All the yarns and yardages needed for all three warps are given here. Instructions for each separate warp will specify how much of each yarn is needed. *Shibui Staccato* (65% superwash merino/30% silk/5% nylon at 1,746 yd/lb [1,597 m/453 g], 191 yd/1.75 oz [175 m/50 g] per skein) in color #111, Bordeaux, 310 yd (283 m) or 2 skeins needed. *Shibui Sock* (100% superwash merino at 1,746 yd/lb (1,597 m/453 g), 191 yd/1.75 oz [175 m/50 g] per skein) in color #1395, Honey, 430 yd (393 m) or 3 skeins needed. *Mountain Meadows Wool Lilura*, 3-ply fingering-weight (50% merino/50% alpaca-merino blend at 2,133 yd/lb [1,950 m/453 g], 200 yd/1.5 oz [183 m/43 g] per skein) in Sorrel, 25 yd (23 m) or 1 skein needed.

Note: The Shibui yarns are quite stretchy and are partially what gives the fabrics such a nice drape. Tie on with firm tension and aim to weave at 14–15 ppi (measured off-tension).

Warp 1: bodice

Warp: Shibui Sock, Honey, 200 yd (183 m) needed.

Weft: Shibui Sock, Honey, 175 yd (160 m) needed, and Mountain Meadows Lilura 25 yd (23 m) needed.

Note: Since you need such a small amount of Lilura, you could use a yarn that you have on hand. However, be sure that the yarn you choose will felt, otherwise you won't get the look shown here.

Weave structure: plain weave and weft floats for bodice.

Warp length: 2 yd (1.8 m), which includes take-up and 24" (61 cm) loom waste. If weaving on a shaft loom, allow 36" (91.5) for loom waste and increase warp yarn yardage by a third.

Warp width: 8¼" (21 cm).

Number of warp ends: 100.

EPI: 12.

PPI: 14–15.

DRAFT FOR BODICE

balance		repeat									
	4	4							4		
			3						3	3	
2						2			2	2	2
1	1	1	1	1	1	1	1				

plain weave

pattern 1 repeat

pattern 2 repeat

WEAVING

Step 1: Weave 12" (30.5 cm) plain weave with Shibui Sock, ending in a down shed.

Step 2: Break off yarn and switch to Lilura.

Step 3: For side, weave 5 repeats of pattern 1 (see draft if weaving on a shaft loom). Pull this weft pattern thread a bit tighter. This, plus the slight felting later, will create the gathered shaping.

Step 4: Weave 9" (23 cm) plain weave with Shibui Sock. End after down shed, break yarn off, and switch to Lilura.

Step 5: For front bodice shaping, weave 3 repeats of pattern 2. Again, pull the pattern weft a bit tighter to create the gathered shaping.

Step 6: With Shibui Sock, weave 9" (23 cm) plain weave, ending in a down shed. Break off yarn.

Step 7: Repeat Step 3 with Lilura for other side.

Step 8: Weave 12" (30.5 cm) plain weave with Shibui Sock.

Pattern 1

Pick-up stick pattern: *2 down, 2 up; repeat from *.

Step 1: Up.

Step 2: Pick-up stick.

Step 3: Up.

Step 4: Down.

Repeat sequence 5 times.

Pattern 2

Pick-up stick pattern: 1 down, *1 up, 3 down; repeat from *. There will be 1 extra thread that will not affect your pattern.

Step 1: Up.

Step 2: Pick-up stick.

Step 3: Up.

Step 4: Pick-up stick.

Step 5: Up.

Step 6: Down.

Repeat 3 times and break off yarn.

Warp 2: skirt

Finished dimensions: 5¼" (13.5 cm) wide × 44" (112 cm) long.

Warp and weft yarns: Shibui Staccato, 140 yd (128 m) needed for warp, and 100 yd (91.5 m) needed for weft.

Weave structure: plain weave.

Warp length: 2 yd (1.8 m), which includes take-up and 24" (61 cm) loom waste. If weaving on a shaft loom, allow 36" (91.5 cm) for loom waste and increase warp yarn yardage by a third.

Warp width: 5½" (14 cm).

Number of warp ends: 66.

EPI: 12.

PPI: 12.

WEAVING

Weave about 48" (122 cm) with Staccato, using an even beat and minding your selvedges that will be the bottom of the "skirt."

Warp 3: straps

Finished dimensions: each strap measures 1¼" (3.2 cm) wide × 18" (45.5 cm) long.

Warp yarn: Shibui Sock, 24 yd (22 m) needed, and Shibui Staccato, 32 yd (29 m) needed.

Weft yarn: Shibui Sock, 36 yd (33 m) needed, and Shibui Staccato, 36 yd (33 m) needed.

Weave structure: plain weave.

Warp length: 2 yd (1.8 m), which includes take-up and 24" (61 cm) loom waste. If weaving on a shaft loom, allow 36" (91. 5 cm) for loom waste and increase warp yarn yardage by a third.

Warp width: 2⅓" (6.5 cm).

Number of warp ends: 28.

EPI: 12.

PPI: 12.

Warp color order for straps:

	3x		end	
Shibui Staccato	4		4	16
Shibui Sock		4		12
			Total ends	28

WEAVING

Use an even beat and pack in tightly. Interlock weft threads and carry them up the edge as you weave (see page 10 for how to interlock using two shuttles). Weave as threaded, 4 picks Shibui Staccato, 4 picks Shibui Sock, repeat.

FABRIC FINISHING FOR ALL THREE FABRICS

Secure all ends with zigzag stitch before washing.

For the bodice: Place in washing machine (we used a front-loading machine) on extreme setting. Check often to supervise progress. Remove from machine, rinse in cold water, and lay flat to dry. Steam-press.

For the other two warps: Handwash in warm water and mild soap. Lay flat to dry and steam-press.

ASSEMBLY

Step 1: Bodice—at either end of the warp, make a ½" (1.3 cm) double rolled hem on wrong side of the fabric. Steam-press and handstitch into place.

Step 2: Attach the skirt to the bodice with machine or handstitching with a ¼" (6 mm) seam allowance. Ease the fabric around the bottom of the bodice, allowing fullness under the arm.

Step 3: Stitch skirt together with a 1" (2.5 cm) seam allowance. Zigzag stitch and trim off any excess as necessary. Steam-press seam allowance under and handstitch into place.

Step 4: Attach the straps. Cut 2 pieces 18½" (47 cm) long. Secure the ends with zigzag stitch. Fold zigzag stitch under ¼" (6 mm) and press. Place the straps 3" (7.5 cm) in from each side, or where desired for good fit, front and back. *Note: Pin first and try on, adjusting as necessary. Handstitch all the way around all four sides where the strap attaches to the garment. Steam-press.*

Step 5: Back closure: Sew a hook and eye to the top of back neck opening. The back will have a slit to the skirt. If desired, add more hooks and eyes to close the gap.

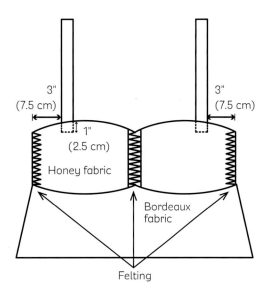

CAMISOLE ASSEMBLY

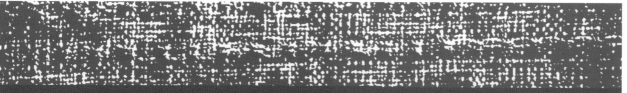

Other fabric ideas

▶ We could see both the bodice and skirt woven in a dainty spot lace in the palest of yellows, accented with pinstriped straps in light pink and yellow. Instead of felting to shape the front and sides, pulled threads could be employed.

▶ Create a fun Fourth of July garment by weaving the top in red and the bottom in white with herringbonepatterned straps in blue and white.

▶ Use your inkle loom for warp-faced straps in bright solid strips to accent a solid fabric.

Alternate styles

▶ Interpret this idea as a strapless dress. You'll most likely need to add gussets at the side to achieve enough flare or weave a longer piece and gather it gently along the top edge. Use elastic at the back for a tight fit—or even weave in the elastic, adjusting the fit during construction (see right).

▶ Weave matching straps and skirt in a lacy weave structure for a baby-doll look.

▶ Use beautiful yarns to weave all the pieces in the same fabric. You might even try your hand at a simple matching wrap skirt for a two-piece dress.

It doesn't have to take a lot of tailoring to make a stylish piece. This charming capelet is basically a long length of fabric with one edge shaped to form a collar. To join the ends, the top corners of the fabric are overlapped and trimmed with a decorative button.

CLASSIC CAPELET

Designed and woven by *Judy Pagels*

The loft of this fingering-weight alpaca/wool yarn combined with Brooks bouquet imparts a knitted appearance to this fabric. Once you get the hang of this technique, it'll progress faster than what you might at first think. The bouquets are loosely executed for a textured look rather than pulled tightly for a lacy effect.

Garment size: small.

Finished dimensions: 18" (45.5 cm) along top, shoulder to shoulder, 12" (30.5 cm) deep.

Equipment: loom with 15" (38 cm) wide weaving width, 10-dent reed, 1 shuttle, tapestry needle.

Notions: 1½" (3.8 cm) button.

Warp and weft yarns: Isager 2 fingering-weight (50% alpaca/50% wool at 2,483 yd/lb [2,270 m/453 g], 273 yd/1.76 oz [250 m/50 g] per skein) in color #47, Blue Gray, 288 yd (263 m) needed for warp and 150 yd (137 m) needed for weft. Two skeins are needed for warp and weft.

Weave structure: plain weave and Brooks bouquet (see how-to on page 71).

Warp length: 2 yd (1.8 m), which includes take-up and 24" (61 cm) loom waste. If weaving on a shaft loom, allow 36" (91.5 cm) for loom waste and increase warp yarn yardage by a third. There is ample room in this warp length to weave a longer fabric to adjust to a larger size.

Warp width: 14½" (37 cm).

Number of warp ends: 144.

EPI: 10.

PPI: about 7.

WEAVING

Following the instructions for making Brooks bouquet, work a row of bouquets using 4 warp ends per bundle. Weave 5 rows of plain weave and repeat. Weave 48" (122 cm) or until the end of the warp.

FABRIC FINISHING

Secure the ends of the fabric with overhand knots. Handwash gently in lukewarm water and lay flat to dry. Lightly steam-press on the wrong side of fabric before assembly. Finished fabric measures 12" × 48" (30.5 × 122 cm).

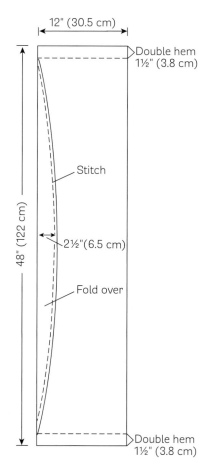

12" (30.5 cm)

Double hem 1½" (3.8 cm)

Stitch

48" (122 cm)

2½"(6.5 cm)

Fold over

Double hem 1½" (3.8 cm)

CLASSIC-CAPELET LAYOUT

BROOKS BOUQUET

Brooks bouquet is one of the speedier finger-control techniques. It is characterized by warp groupings that give a lacy effect as well as little windowpanes between each bouquet. In Brooks bouquet, the groups are wrapped on an open shed on the top threads only. The "incidentals" are the warp threads on the bottom of the shed that appear between the bundles. After each bouquet row, change the shed and weave a row of plain weave to lock the bouquets into place. Working across from your dominant side will be easiest. Generally, at least a couple of picks of plain weave are woven between each row of bouquets.

Making Brooks bouquet

Step 1: Open the shed. Working right to left (or from the direction of your dominant hand), insert your shuttle into the shed as far as your bouquet is wide. Bring your shuttle to the surface. For this sample, each group is 4 raised warp threads (**Figure 1**).

Step 2: Travel left to right over this same group (4 raised warp threads) and reinsert your shuttle into the shed right to left (the same direction you began). Travel through the shed for a total of 8 warp threads and bring the shuttle to the surface (**Figure 2**).

Step 3: Pull tight to cinch up the bundle (**Figure 3**). Repeat Steps 1–3. (*Note: This is the classic way to make Brooks bouquet. For this project, we left the bundle loosely tied.*)

Step 4: When you reach the other selvedge, change sheds and weave back to the other side (**Figure 4**).

Tip: For uniform bundles, try to keep tension on your working end. You may find it helpful to pinch the previous knot with one hand as you bring the shuttle out of the shed for the next bundle, thus preventing the previous bouquet from loosening up.

To learn more about making Brooks bouquet, see *The Weaver's Idea Book*, pages 59–63.

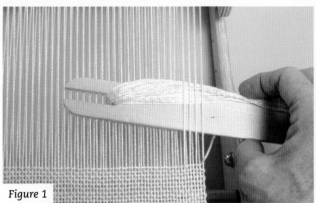

Figure 1

Figure 2

Figure 3

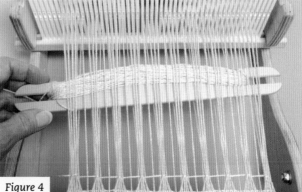

Figure 4

ASSEMBLY

Step 1: Sew the first hem. Machine stitch the end of the fabric just above the first pick of a row of bouquets. To prevent the fabric from pulling, use a long machine stitch. Trim off waste. With the wrong side up, make a double rolled hem using the bouquets as a guide. Lightly press and pin. Using the project yarn, handsew the hem in between the bouquets to preserve the open spaces. Stitch up the sides of the hem for tidy edges.

Step 2: Determine fit. Using a mirror or a friend, fold over the top edge for the collar. Drape the fabric across the shoulders to determine fit and mark the edge of the unfinished edge with a large pin along one of the bouquet rows.

Step 3: Sew the second hem as you did for the first one.

Step 4: Make collar. Place the fabric right side up on a flat surface. Mark the center along the top edge and using the bouquet sections as a guide, fold back 4 rows (2½" [6.5 cm]) and pin. Fold back 1 row (bouquet bundle) at either end of the top edge and pin. Then pin along this edge to form a curved neckline increasing the number of folded bouquets to the widest point. With the project yarn, secure the collar by starting at one end and handstitching between 2 rows of Brooks bouquet bundles, 1 row from the selvedge edge.

Step 5: Add the closure. On a flat surface with the front of the capelet facing you, fold the right side (left side facing you) over the left, about 2½" (6.5 cm) and secure with pins. Try on and adjust the closure overlap as needed. Line up the fold-over with the grain of the cloth. Secure around all edges with project yarn. Finish off with a decorative button.

A note about sizing: If increasing the warp width, work in multiples of 8.

Other fabric ideas

▸ Weave a big plaid in a lofty wool yarn and secure with a large pin, Scottish-style.

▸ Rows of handworked leno alternated with stripes of plain weave woven in raw silk would result in an elegant fabric, perfect for evening wear.

▸ Use a highly textured novelty yarn for warp and weft for an easy-weave casual look. Accent with a large wooden button.

Alternate styles

▸ By weaving this piece wider, you can create a longer cape. The fringe at the bottom edge would need to be woven along one selvedge by spacing 2 warp threads 3"–4" (7.5–10 cm) away from the edge of the main warp (see top, right).

▸ Wear the button on the side, not down the front (see bottom, right).

Fine yarns sett at 12 ends per inch are woven to create an open fabric, which is then washed well (with careful oversight!) to heavily full the yarns to create this lovely drapey fabric. The top edge is folded down and accordion pleated for a collar.

CAPE WITH COLLAR

Designed by *Jane Patrick and Sara Goldenberg*; woven by *Gail Matthews*

Fine yarns heavily fulled result in a light, dreamy-soft fabric. When threading the warp, we gradually increased the width of the accent yarn stripes for a subtle gradation, using the closest-set stripes for the collar. During weaving, we carried the accent yarn up the selvedges to create little picots at the edge. A hook-and-eye closure is the finishing touch. If capes aren't your thing, you could use this fabric design for a scarf or shawl.

Garment size: medium.

Finished dimensions: 17½" (44.5 cm) from neckline to bottom of cape, 75" (190.5 cm) around the bottom edge, 22" (56 cm) neck circumference.

Equipment: loom with 25" (63.5 cm) weaving width, 12-dent reed, 2 shuttles, washing machine, sewing machine.

Notions: 1 hook-and-eye closure.

Warp yarn: *Nirvana from Filatura Di Crosa, Tahki-Stacy Charles Inc.* (100% superwash merino wool at 6,764 yd/lb [6,185 m/453 g], 372 yd/.88 oz [340 m/25 g] per ball) in color 35, gray, 700 yd (640 m) or 2 balls needed. *Gioiello Fancy from Filatura Di Crosa, Tahki-Stacy Charles Inc.*(30% kid mohair/30% wool/20% polyamide/10% cotton/10% polyester at 1,829 yd/lb [1,672 m/453 g], 220 yd/1.75 oz [201 m/50 g] per ball) in color 69 Tiger Eye, 70 yd (64 m) or 1 ball needed.

Weft yarn: *Superior from Filatura Di Crosa, Tahki-Stacy Charles Inc.* (70% cashmere/25% silk/5% merino wool at 5,964 yd/lb [5,453 m/453 g], 328 yd/.88 oz [300 m/25 g] per ball) in color 73 Charcoal, 465 yd (425 m) or 2 balls needed. You will also need the same Gioiello used in the warp, 95 yards (87 m).

Weave structure: plain weave.

Warp length: 2½ yd (2.3 m), which includes take-up and 24" (61 cm) loom waste. If weaving on a shaft loom, allow 36" (91.5 cm) loom waste and increase your warp yarn yardage by a third.

Warp width: 23⅓" (59.5 cm).

Number of warp ends: 280.

EPI: 12.

PPI: 12.

Warp color order:

	4x	4x	4x	4x	4x	4x	4x	
Gioiello	1	1	1	1	1	1	1	28
Nirvana	3	5	7	9	11	13	15	252
						Total warp ends		280

WEAVING

Weave 5 rows Superior and 1 row Gioiello; repeat for the entire length of the warp. Carry the Gioiello up the selvedges. This will give a scalloped look to the edges, which are left untouched in the final finishing and assembly. Use a light, even beat and mind your selvedges—they're both going to show. You want this fabric to be quite open. Check the fabric often to make sure your beat remains consistently at 12 ppi.

FABRIC FINISHING

Secure ends of weaving with overhand knots. Fill a sink with hot water and Dawn detergent. Submerge the fabric in the water and let it soak for about 30 minutes. Agitate by hand, squeezing, not wringing, the fabric to full it. Rinse in warm water. Place the fabric in the dryer with a couple of towels. Use the hottest setting and check often to monitor progress. When sufficiently fulled, remove the fabric from the dryer and lay it flat to dry. Steam-press using a press cloth and lots of steam and pressure.

ASSEMBLY

Step 1: Zigzag stitch on either end of cloth. Cut off fringe and make ¼" (6 mm) double rolled hems on both ends of the fabric. Steam-press, pin, and machine stitch into place.

Step 2: On the edge with the densest novelty yarn stripes, create a collar by folding over the top 3" (7.5 cm) of fabric onto the right side. Pin into place.

Step 3: To make the pleats, working on the right side of the fabric, start ¼" (6 mm) in from the front edge and make 2" (5 cm) accordion pleats ½" (1.3 cm) apart all the way around the edge, leaving ¼" (6 mm) at the end to match the other side. Pin vertically as you go. (See notes below on making accordion pleats.)

Step 4: Handstitch the pleats into place with a backstitch (see page 12 for how-to) all the way across the top edge, ⅛" (3 mm) down from the top.

Step 5: Attach the hook-and-eye closure at the top edge.

ACCORDION PLEATS

You can measure and mark the points with pins all the way across the collar and then begin folding in this way: point 1 folds onto point 2, point 3 folds onto point 4, and so on.

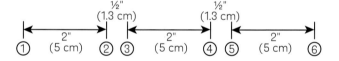

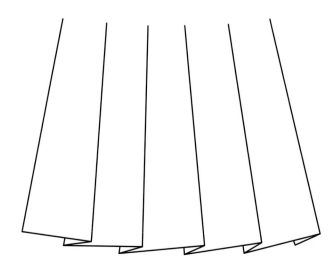

Other fabric ideas

▶ Use Brooks bouquet as shown in the Classic Capelet, except pull the bundles very tightly for an open weave. Use a crisp yarn such as a linen blend or pearl cotton to help define the groupings.

▶ Accent the collar by threading the collar in a contrasting yarn, say pale blue for the body and dark blue for the collar. Weave with a neutral weft such as a medium gray to blend it all together.

▶ For vertical stripes, thread up a plain warp and weave across in a narrow stripe pattern in earthy colors.

Alternate styles

▶ Weave a separate piece for a stand-up collar. Choose one of the accent yarns from the body of the cape and use it to weave a solid-colored fabric to contrast with the main fabric.

▶ Weave a wider fabric or two separate pieces for a two-layered look. Use pulled warps to gather the fabric at neckline (see right).

▶ A narrow strip of fabric with pulled warps along one edge can be fashioned into a stylish collar.

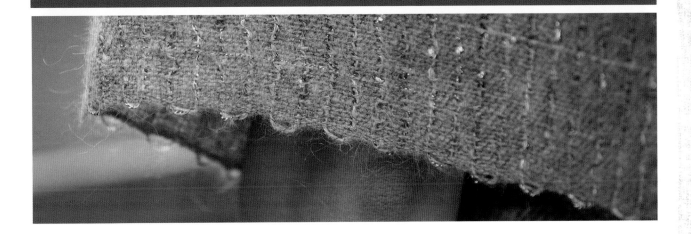

A shrug is about the easiest garment construction possible. We'd put it somewhere between a shawl and a jacket. It acts like a shawl, but because it has sleeves, it stays on and is most wearable. For this shrug, we added rope trim detailing at the neck and sleeves. Turning up the cuffs adds a bit of tailoring, as does folding down the back neck for a collar of sorts—simple details that lend style.

FALL BLAZE SHRUG

Designed and woven by *Sara Goldenberg*

A shrug is essentially a long piece of fabric that is folded lengthwise with the ends stitched up to create sleeves. For this piece, we've used a crepe yarn that is squishy, making a soft, flowy garment. Because it is somewhat elastic in nature, the crepe yarn is easy to pull too much during weaving. Use moderate tension on the warp so as not to stretch the yarn excessively. When weaving, insert the weft in the shed but don't pull on it. Otherwise, this is a dream to weave.

You'll find that there is quite a lot of shrinkage with this yarn. After weaving, the fabric measured 24" × 63" (61 × 160 cm). After washing, it measured 20" × 60" (51 × 152.5 cm).

Garment size: medium.

Finished dimensions: sleeves measure 20" (51 cm]) in circumference. Length from sleeve end to sleeve end is 49½" (125.5 cm).

Equipment: loom with 25" (63.5 cm) weaving width, 1 shuttle, 8-dent reed, rope machine (optional), sewing machine (optional).

Warp yarn: *Mountain Colors Half Crepe* (100% merino wool at 1,680 yd/lb [1,536 m/453 g], 630 yd/6 oz [576 m/170 g] per skein) in Hummingbird, 250 yd (229 m) or 1 skein needed. *Mountain Colors Merino Ribbon* (80% superfine merino wool/20% nylon at 980 yd/lb [896 m/453 g], 245 yd/4 oz [224 m/113 g] per skein) in Spring Eclipse, 245 yd (224 m) or 1 skein needed.

Weft yarn: *Mountain Colors Half Crepe* (100% merino wool at 1,680 yd/lb [1,536 m/453 g], 630 yd/6 oz [576 m/170 g] per skein) in Marigold, 420 yd (384 m) or 1 skein needed.

Trim: *Mountain Colors 4/8's Wool* (100% wool at 1,145 yd/lb [1,047 m/453 g], 250 yd/3.5 oz [229 m/100 g] per skein) in Hummingbird, 125 yd (114 m) or 1 skein needed.

Weave structure: plain weave.

Warp length: 2½ yd (2.3 m), which includes take-up and 24" (61 cm) loom waste.

If weaving on a shaft loom, allow 36" (91.5 cm) for loom waste and increase warp yarn yardage by a third.

Warp width: 25" (63.5 cm).

Number of warp ends: 200 (100 each of Half Crepe and Merino Ribbon).

Warping plan: alternate Crepe and Merino Ribbon, sleying the ribbon in the slots.

EPI: 8.

PPI: 9.

FIT NOTES

The fit is flexible, though generally you want a loose, easy fit. The width of your loom will determine the circumference of the sleeves. We used a loom 25" (63.5 cm) wide and folded the fabric in half lengthwise. If you have a narrower loom, you could weave this garment in 2 pieces, sewing a center seam (instead of folding lengthwise). If you choose to weave a wider garment, you might want to taper the sleeves so as not to have excessively wide, floppy sleeves. Other ideas: gather the sleeve ends with knitting or weave a short length of fabric for short sleeves.

WEAVING

Begin and end weaving with hemstitching. Weave at about 9 ppi using an even beat for 63" (160 cm) or until the end of the warp.

FABRIC FINISHING

Handwash in hot, soapy water. Lay flat to dry and lightly steam-press.

ASSEMBLY

Step 1: Make a ½" (1.3 cm) double rolled hem at either end of the cloth. Hand or machine stitch.

Step 2: Fold the fabric in half lengthwise with the rolled hem facing out.

Step 3: Measure 15" (38 cm) from either end along the seam edge. With wrong sides together, sew either by hand or machine with the ⅛" (3 mm) seam on the

outside. Butt edges together with minimal overlap to keep bulk to a minimum. This allows for a roughly 26" (66 cm) neck-shoulder opening.

Step 4: On the right side, fold up sleeve ends 2½" (6.5 cm), steam-press, and tack in place by hand.

Step 5: Along the neckline, fold the top edge down on the right side to create a collar. The thickest point at the centerline is 2½" (6.5 cm). Taper to the edge and tack down by hand.

Step 6: With the accent yarn, make a 75" (190.5 cm) long rope or braided trim (see page 83 for how to make a rope using a rope machine).

Step 7: Stitch the rope around the cuff and collar by hand. Secure with overhand knots at the beginning and end of each trim piece.

VARIATION

Designed and woven by Sara Goldenberg
We used the same painted wool crepe yarn for warp and weft for this little topper, which we accented with little pom-poms in the same yarn. Folding back the neckline for a collar adds a bit of shaping. Yarns are from Mountain Colors.

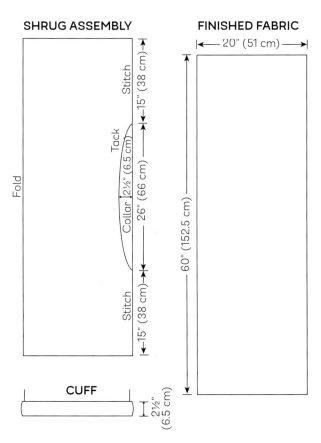

SHRUG ASSEMBLY

FINISHED FABRIC

Other fabric ideas

▸ This design lends itself to fuzzy yarns. Check your stash and thread up an assortment of novelty yarns in similar colors and weave with a single novelty yarn for weft. Thread the bulkiest yarns in the slots.

▸ Create a summery wrap by threading up a natural bouclé yarn in the warp and crossing with the same yarn in the weft. Trim cuffs with a shiny rayon ribbon.

▸ For a tailored look, weave a large check in silver-gray and dark charcoal. If weaving 2 pieces that will need to be matched along the shoulder, use an even beat and measure often.

Alternate styles

▸ Weave a short length of fabric for an elbow-length shrug. Use the warp ends as fringe. Think Mexican fiesta.

▸ For a coatlike look, weave a wider fabric, fold over the top edge for a collar, and give the sleeves a good taper (see top, right).

▸ Taper the sleeves and add broad knitted trims in a contrasting color (see bottom, right).

MAKING ROPE ON THE INCREDIBLE ROPE MACHINE

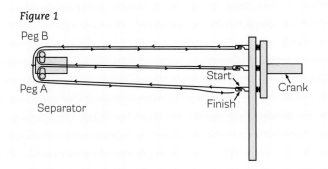

Figure 1

Peg B

Peg A

Separator

Start

Finish

Crank

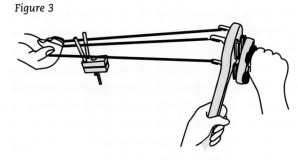

Figure 3

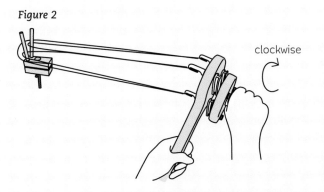

Figure 2

clockwise

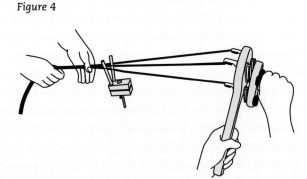

Figure 4

Step 1. Clamp the separator to a table top (**Figure 1**). Determine the desired length of the rope and then tie the yarns to the first hook on the Rope Machine. Following the diagram, carry the yarns around Peg A, around the middle hook on the Rope Machine, around Peg B, then around the last hook on the Rope Machine, and finally return around the outside of Pegs B and A, ending where you began. There should be two lines of yarn from each peg. For a thicker rope, repeat the process as many times as desired.

Step 2. Turn the handle crank to add twist to the strands (**Figure 2**). Turn the handle crank in the direction of the twist in the yarn (clockwise for most yarns) to add twist, keeping the yarns taut as you crank. The more turns, the tighter the finished rope will be. As the yarns become more twisted, they will "take up" and shorten the rope strands. Crank until the

twist is so tight that when tension is released, the yarns kink back onto themselves.

Step 3. Pull the 3 strands slowly away from the separator to twist them back onto themselves to make the rope (**Figures 3** and **4**). Take hold of the yarns at the back of the separator and pull them slowly, evenly, and smoothly, allowing them to twist together in a counterclockwise direction (opposite what you did in the first step). It is helpful to have a second person hold the Rope Machine while you pull the yarn through the separator. Add more twist, if needed, by cranking clockwise. As the Rope Machine moves closer to the separator, crank a few clockwise turns to keep the strands tightly twisted. When the Rope Machine reaches the separator, slip the 3 strands off the hooks and tie an overhand knot in the end to secure them.]

Our new take on the traditional ruana gives this ethnic-style garment a more finished look. Wear it open, belt it, or throw one end over your shoulder for a bit of drama.

GOOD EARTH RUANA

Designed by *Jane Patrick and Sara Goldenberg*; woven by *David Pipinich*

This thick, comfy wrap is something you'll turn to again and again. We used a mixed warp and wove with a single wool yarn. To keep this design affordable, we used an acrylic knitting yarn for every other thread in the warp. The fabric was "designed in the reed," where we sleyed a variety of yarns in a hit-and-miss fashion (alternating with the acrylic knitting yarn). This is a great project for using up all your little yarn dibby dabs. We've updated this traditional design by cutting a neck hole, turning the front panels under for a finished look, and adding a bulky rolled hem at the outside edges. We've hemmed the bottom, but you could also leave fringe for a more casual look.

We used six yarns in the warp. Though we purchased new yarns, this fabric design also lends itself to digging into your stash. When weaving on a rigid-heddle loom, you will most likely need to weave this project on two separate warps.

Garment size: one size fits all.

Finished dimensions: 32" (81.5 cm) from shoulder to hem, 31" (79 cm) edge to edge.

Equipment: loom with 20" (51 cm) weaving width, 8-dent reed, 1 shuttle, sewing machine.

Warp yarns: *Plymouth Yarn Encore Chunky* (75% acrylic/25% wool at 654 yd/lb [598 m/453 g], 143 yd/3.5 oz [131 m/100 g] per ball]) in color #1405, gray-green, 480 yd (439 m) or 4 balls needed. *Tahki Yarns Juno* (97% alpaca/3% nylon at 770 yd/lb [704 m/453 g], 84 yd/1.75 oz [77 m/50 g] per ball) in color #07, Paprika, 160 yd (146 m) or 2 balls needed. Classic *Elite Yarns Liberty Wool* (100% washable wool) at 1,115 yd/lb [1,019 m/453 g], 122 yd/1.75 oz [112 m/50 g] per ball) in printed color #7899, Cloudy Dawn, 165 yd (151 m) or 2 balls needed. *Trendsetter Checkmate* (80% polyamide/20% nylon ribbon at 640 yd/lb [585 m/453 g], 70 yd/1.75 oz [64 m/50 g] per ball) in color #603, Harvest, 100 yd (91 m) or 2 balls needed. *Lorna's Laces Pearl* (51% silk/49% bamboo at 636 yd/lb [582 m/453 g], 220 yd/3.5 oz [201 m/100 g] per skein) in color 50NS, Poppy, 30 yd (27.5 m) or 1 skein needed.

Ironstone Big Loop Mohair (90% mohair/5% wool/5% nylon at 600 yd/lb [549 m/453 g], available on 6 lb cones) in Shade 251 (E), 36 yd (33 m) needed.

Substitution note: Only small amounts of Lorna's Laces and Ironstone are used. This would be a good place to substitute a yarn from your stash. Try a shiny pearl cotton or Tencel as a substitute for the Lorna's

Laces Pearl. You want something shiny here. For the Big Mohair Loop, try a textured yarn that will add a bit of fuzz to the surface of the fabric.

Weft yarn: *Brown Sheep Lamb's Pride, Worsted* (85% wool/15% mohair at 760 yd/lb [695 m/453 g], 190 yd/4 oz [173 m/113 g] per skein]) in color #M-07, Sable, 725 yd (663 m) or 4 skeins needed.

Weave structure: plain weave.

Warp length: If weaving on a rigid heddle loom, because of the thickness of the yarns, you'll need to warp the loom twice; each warp is 3 yd (2.75 m) long, which includes take-up and 24" (61 cm) loom waste. When warping twice, if you want both sides to be the same, you'll need to make notes about the threading order of the warp yarns for your first warp.

Note: You'll need to allow about 50 more yd (46 m) of warp if threading up 2 warps. If you're weaving on a shaft loom, you can thread 1 warp 5½ yd (5 m) long.

Warp width: 20" (51 cm).

Number of warp ends: 160.

Warping instructions: Measure the following: 80 ends *Encore Chunky*, 26 ends *Juno*, 27 ends *Liberty Wool*, 16 ends *Checkmate*, 5 ends *Pearl*, 6 ends *Big Loop Mohair*. Measure

each yarn separately on the warping board. Thread *Encore Chunky* in every hole and then randomly sley the other yarns, spreading them out across the total width and making sure all of the slots are filled.

EPI: 8.

PPI: 7.

WEAVING

Wind a shuttle with Lamb's Pride Worsted and weave with a gentle beat. Advance the warp often to help keep an even beat. Weave 75" (190.5 cm) for each panel or to the end of the warp.

FABRIC FINISHING

Cut the fabric in half to make it easier to wash. Zigzag stitch on either side of center before cutting. Secure all of the raw ends with long zigzag stitching to prevent raveling. Machine wash in hot, soapy water. Add about 2 tablespoons of hair conditioner during the rinsing process and let the fabric soak for 5 minutes. Rinse in warm water and air-dry. Steam-press. There was virtually no shrinkage in the finishing process.

ASSEMBLY

Step 1: Make 1" (2.5 cm) double rolled hems across the bottom of the front panels, making sure the 2 panels are even in length. Heavily steam-press (the fabric is bulky and steaming will help keep the fabric in place) and then pin before stitching. If using a machine, stitch slowly over ribbon areas.

Step 2: Stack the panels one on top of the other, right sides together so that the pattern is matching (this way the sewn fabric will be a mirror image panel to panel).

LAYOUT

70" (177.5 cm)

19" (48.5 cm)

Cut 2 panels   19" X 70" (48.5 x 177.5 cm)

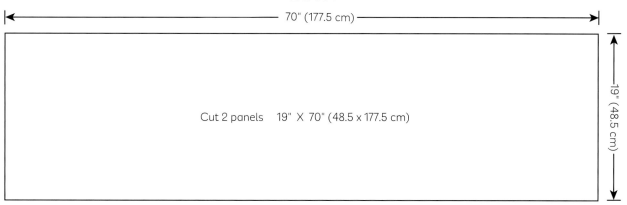

NECK HOLE

7" (18 cm)

5" (12.5 cm)

Cut along
zigzag

Snip   Snip

 〜 = Zigzag

✂ = Cut

☐ = 1" (2.5 cm)

7" (18 cm)

3"   3"
(7.5 cm)   (7.5 cm)

½" (1.3 cm)   ½" (1.3 cm)
hem   hem

5"
(12.5 cm)

32" (81.5 cm)

15"   15"
(38 cm)   (38 cm)

- - - - Stitch from bottom up to neck-hole

RUANA ASSEMBLY

Sew the back seam with a ⅝" (1.5 cm) seam allowance for 34" (86.5 cm). Steam-press the seam open.

Step 3: Make a 1" (2.5 cm) double rolled hem across the back bottom. Heavily steam-press and pin before stitching.

Step 4: Cut the neck hole using the template (see diagram on page 87). To better manage all of the fabric, we cut the template in half vertically and then cut the neck hole first on one side and then the other. Pin the straight edge of the template 1" (2.5 cm) to the back of the top of the back seam. Pin template into place and then zigzag stitch around the template before cutting. (Because the ruana is open in the front, it's easiest to stitch one side then the next instead of trying to do the entire neck hole at once.) Repeat on the other side. Next, zigzag stitch a second line. Stitch inside the first zigzag

row following the same curve of the template but ¾" (2 cm) in. Secure with straight stitch around snip lines (see diagram on page 87). Cut away cloth inside the inner ring. Snip between straight-stitch areas stopping ⅛" (3 mm) before edge of outer zigzag ring. Create a rolled hem all the way around the neck. Steam-press. The outer zigzag row is the outer edge of the neck hole. Pin the hem and stitch into place. Steam-press.

Step 5: Finish the front opening by folding the front edges under ½" (1.3 cm) from the end of the neck notch to the bottom of the fabric. Press and tack into place by hand.

Step 6: Finish the outside edges with a chunky rolled hem. Using 4" (10 cm) of cloth, roll the fabric along the edges for a 1" wide (2.5 cm) chunky roll. Pin, then tack into place by hand. Do not press.

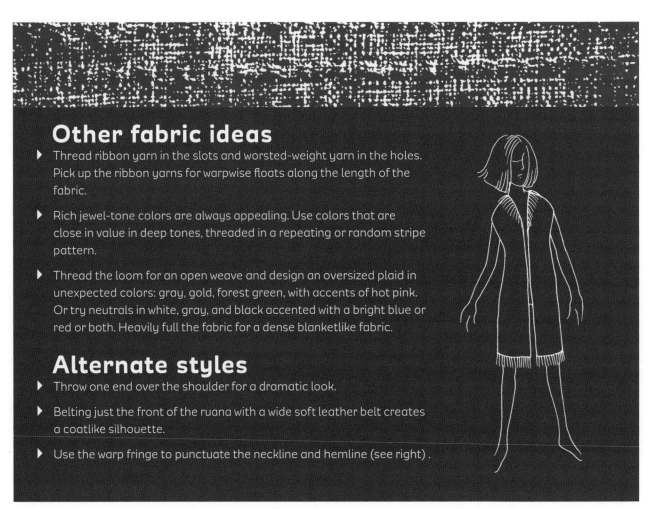

Other fabric ideas

▸ Thread ribbon yarn in the slots and worsted-weight yarn in the holes. Pick up the ribbon yarns for warpwise floats along the length of the fabric.

▸ Rich jewel-tone colors are always appealing. Use colors that are close in value in deep tones, threaded in a repeating or random stripe pattern.

▸ Thread the loom for an open weave and design an oversized plaid in unexpected colors: gray, gold, forest green, with accents of hot pink. Or try neutrals in white, gray, and black accented with a bright blue or red or both. Heavily full the fabric for a dense blanketlike fabric.

Alternate styles

▸ Throw one end over the shoulder for a dramatic look.

▸ Belting just the front of the ruana with a wide soft leather belt creates a coatlike silhouette.

▸ Use the warp fringe to punctuate the neckline and hemline (see right).

Here's a top that is sure to become a wardrobe staple. Wear it long over tights with just a slight gathering of the waist or blouson-style with a tightly pulled waistline. The shaping is achieved by threading in a draw cord at the shoulders and waistline.

FLAME LACE TOP

Designed by *Jane Patrick and Sara Goldenberg*; woven by *David Pipinich*

A block lace weave structure provides background texture for this long, flowing top. We doubled fine yarns in the warp and weft. The space-dyed hemp warp plays against a doubled, shiny Tencel weft, one end spaced-dyed, the other solid, for a fabric that is ever changing.

Garment size: medium.

Finished dimensions: 21" (53.5 cm) wide by 38" (96.5 cm) shoulder to hem.

Equipment: loom with 24" (61 cm) weaving width, 12-dent reed, 1 shuttle , sewing machine.

Warp yarn: *Interlacements 2-ply Hemp* (100% hemp at 4,190 yd/lb [3,831 m/453 g], 2,095 yd/8 oz [1,915 m/ 227 g] per skein), in Colorado Treasures, 2,016 yd (1,843 m) or 1 skein needed. *Note: All ends are used doubled.*

Weft yarn: *WEBS/ Valley Fibers 8/2 Tencel* (100% Tencel at 3,360 yd/ lb [3,072 m/453 g], available on 1 lb [453 g] cones) in Fire and Pompeii, 900 yd (823 m) needed of each color or 1 cone each. *Note: These yarns are used together as one.*

Notions: 4 yd (3.6 m) of dark blue ⅛" (3 mm) wide ribbon.

Weave structure: block lace.

Warp length: 3½ yd (3.2 m), which includes take-up and 24" (61 cm) loom waste. If weaving on a shaft loom, allow 36" (91.5 cm) for loom waste and increase warp yarn yardage by a third.

Warp width: 24" (61 cm).

Number of warp ends: 288 working ends (576 total ends). *Note: Ends are used doubled.*

EPI: 12.

PPI: 12.

Note: Fire and Pompeii are used doubled in the weft and yield 12 ppi.

PICK-UP PATTERN:

Pick-up stick A: *2 up, 2 down; repeat from *.

Pick-up stick B: *2 down, 2 up; repeat from *.

Step 1: Down.

Step 2: Up and pick-up stick A.

Step 3: Down.

Step 4: Up and pick-up stick A.

Step 5: Down.

Step 6: Up.

Step 7: Down.

Step 8: Up and pick-up stick B.

Step 9: Down.

Step 10: Up and pick-up stick B.

Step 11: Down.

Step 12: Up.

Repeat these 12 steps for pattern.

DRAFT

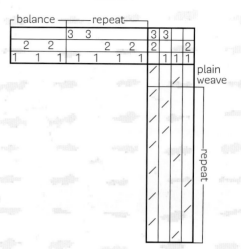

WEAVING

Wind Fire and Pompeii together on a shuttle and beat at 12 ppi. This will be a loose beat. Do not overbeat, as this will produce a stiff fabric. Weave pattern for 90" (229 cm) or until the end of the warp.

FABRIC FINISHING

Secure the ends with zigzag stitch. Handwash in warm water with mild detergent. Lay flat to dry. Steam-press on medium.

ASSEMBLY

Neck-hole

Step 1: Find center of the cloth both lengthwise and widthwise.

Step 2: Pin down neck-hole template so the center of the template is on the center of the cloth.

Step 3: Secure around the edges of the template with zigzag stitch.

Step 4: Stitch again 1" (2.5 cm) inside the first zigzag stitching.

Step 5: Mark the edge of the inner circle about every 1½" (3.8 cm). Secure with straight stitch on either side of the snip lines.

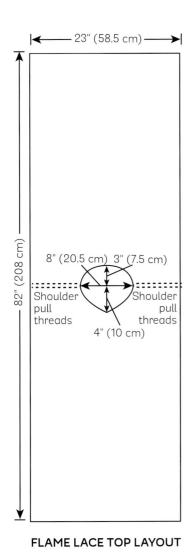

FLAME LACE TOP LAYOUT

23" (58.5 cm)

82" (208 cm)

8" (20.5 cm)   3" (7.5 cm)

Shoulder pull threads   Shoulder pull threads

4" (10 cm)

8" (20.5 cm)

3" (7.5 cm)

4" (10 cm)

--- = Stitch
ᴡ = Zigzag
✄ = Cut
☐ = 1" (2.5 cm)

Note: after stitching, cut out neck-hole.

NECK-HOLE LAYOUT

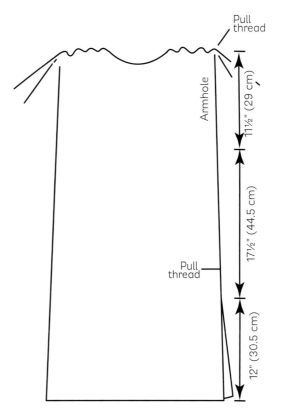

Pull thread

Armhole

Pull thread

11½" (29 cm)

17½" (44.5 cm)

12" (30.5 cm)

FLAME LACE ASSEMBLY LAYOUT

Step 6: Cut out centermost circle (it will be small).

Step 7: Leaving all zigzag stitching intact, cut snip lines toward the outer circle stopping ⅛" (3 mm) away from it. These cuts will allow you to fold over chunks of the circle to create a double rolled hem along the neckline.

Step 8: Fold the neckline flaps to create a double rolled hem. Steam-press in place, hand baste, and then machine stitch. Machine stitch the outermost edge of neck-hole, then tack the hem to the ground cloth by hand so it lies flat.

Shoulders

Step 1: Needle weave ribbon at the bases of the long hemp warp floats, starting from the outside edge, turning at the neck-hole, and needle weaving back to the edge under the next group of warp floats.

Step 2: Use 20" (51 cm) of ribbon for each shoulder.

Step 3: Leave 3" (7.5 cm) tails on either end and pull tails to cinch shoulder to desired width. Tie a square knot and make a bow or leave loose.

Armholes, side seams, and waist tie

Step 1: With right sides together, measure 11½" (29 cm) down from the shoulder. This will be your armhole.

Step 2: Pin and sew the sides with a ⅝" (1.5 cm) seam allowance from this point for 17½" (44.5 cm).

Step 3: Insert ribbon 2" (5 cm) above end of the side seam in the same way you did for the shoulder seams. Weave the ribbon all the way around and pull the string to gather, then tie in a bow.

Step 4: Make ½" (1.3 cm) double rolled hems around the bottom edge. Steam-press and pin before stitching. Make sure the stitch length is long enough so that the cloth isn't pulled by the sewing machine. Alternately, sew by hand.

Step 5: Fold 1" (2.5 cm) of cloth under all the way around armholes, steam-press, and tack into place by hand.

Other fabric ideas

▸ This garment can be taken in so many directions: light, airy fabrics for summer or dense fabrics for winter.

▸ Weave this in a spot lace pattern using solid blue in the warp and solid green in the weft. The float patterns will accent either the blue or green depending on whether you make warp floats or weft floats.

▸ On a solid warp, blend the colors from dark to light, starting at the hemline and moving up to the shoulders; repeat the color progression in reverse on the back, blending from light at the shoulders to dark at the hemline.

Alternate styles

▸ Try a shorter look with an open front. Either weave 2 narrower panels for the front or cut a wide panel down the middle. Again, pull cords at the shoulders and waist to add shaping (see top, right).

▸ Weave 2 panels but insert the pull cord higher for a princess style and don't pull the shoulders (see bottom, right).

▸ By weaving the panels even longer, you can create a dress. Provide shaping at the waist with cording. Change the neckline with a scoop neck and don't pull the shoulders.

We threaded pairs of green mohair warps across the warp width for vertical accents along the length of the tunic. To bring the color to the surface, we let these yarns float along the length of the fabric. We used the same green mohair for weft to accent the waistband and collar.

TURTLENECK TUNIC

Designed and woven by *Sara Goldenberg*

This simple tunic is just two rectangles, slightly shaped, with a contrasting waistband and oversized collar. The main yarn used for the tunic is a chenille wrapped with a mohair loop that has a lot of give, making for a comfy fit. This casual topper will become a wardrobe staple.

Garment size: small.

Finished dimensions: from the top of the shoulder to the bottom of the hem: 25" (63.5 cm), From side seam to side seam: 18" (45.5 cm). Folded collar measures 11½" (29 cm) wide × 12" (30.5 cm) deep, which includes 4" (10 cm) for the fold over.

Equipment: loom with at least a 20" (51 cm) weaving width, 10-dent reed, 1 or 2 shuttles, sewing machine.

Warp and weft yarn:
Velvet by Interlacements (70% rayon/30% mohair at 700 yd/lb [640 m/453 g], available on 700 yd/1 lb cones [640 m/453 g]), 800 yards (732 m) or 2 cones of Navy Blue needed. *Silk Cloud by Shibui Knits Yarn* (60% kid mohair/40% silk at 6,000 yd/lb [5486 m/453 g], 330 yd/.88 oz per skein [301 m/25 g]), 379 yd (346.5 m) or 2 skeins of #2024 Lime needed.

Note: Mohair is doubled in the warp.

Weave structure: plain weave with paired warp floats.

Warp length: 3 yd (2.75 m), which includes take-up and allows 24" (61 cm) loom waste. Warp width: 25" (63.5 cm). When weaving on a shaft loom, allow 36" (91.5 cm) loom waste and increase the warp yarn yardage by a third.

Warp Width: 20" (51 cm).

Total number of warp ends: 232.
Note: Mohair is used double.

EPI: 10.

PPI: 9.

PICK-UP PATTERN:

Pick up the mohair warp threads 4 down, *2 up, 4 down; repeat from *.

Step 1: Down.

Step 2: Up and pick-up stick.

Step 3: Down.

Step 4: Up and pick- up stick.

Step 5: Down.

Step 6: Up.

Repeat Steps 1–6.

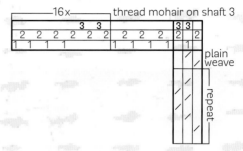

TURTLENECK TUNIC DRAFT

Warp color order:

	Repeat 16x			End		
Velvet	9		1	8		168
Mohair*		2		2		64
				Total ends		232

Note: When threading this pattern in a rigid-heddle reed, be sure to thread the mohair yarns in the slots. Begin threading in a hole.

*64 actual ends and 32 working ends. (Mohair is doubled in the slots.)

WEAVING

Step 1: Weave waistband 3" (7.5 cm) in plain weave using mohair.

Step 2: Weave 25" (63.5 cm) for the body in warp float pattern using Velvet.

Step 3: Weave 14" (35.5 cm) in plain weave with mohair for the turtleneck.

Step 4: Weave a 2" (5 cm) spacer with scrap yarn.

Step 5: Repeat Steps 1–3 for the back of the garment, measuring carefully to match the front.

FABRIC FINISHING

Secure edges with overhand knots and handwash in warm, soapy water. Lay flat to dry.

ASSEMBLY

Construction

Step 1: Zigzag stitch between the front and back panels and cut them apart.

Step 2: Sew a ¼" (6 mm) double rolled hem on the bottom of the waistband edge on the front and back.

Step 3: To shape the turtleneck, find the widthwise center at the bottom edge of the turtleneck on the front and mark with a pin. Measure out from the center 5¾" (14.5 cm) to the right and 5¾" (14.5 cm) to the left of the center pin and mark with pins. This will create an 11" (28 cm) wide turtleneck. From these pins, on both the front and the back, mark the length of the turtleneck with a row of pins. Zigzag stitch up the turtleneck along the inside of the pin line on both the front and the back.

Step 4: Zigzag stitch across the shoulders from the base of the turtleneck to the selvedge edge on both the front and the back (see illustration).

Step 5: Cut out the excess rectangles on both sides of the turtleneck (roughly 4" [10 cm] wide on each side by 14" [35.5 cm] long).

Step 6: On both the front and the back, create a ¼" (6 mm) double rolled hem at the top of the turtleneck. The hem should roll toward the front (outside of the tunic) so that when the turtleneck is folded over, the hem will be on the inside.

Step 7: With right sides together, sew shoulder seams using a ⅝" (1.5 cm) seam allowance.

Step 8: With right sides together, sew side seams using a ⅝" (1.5 cm) seam allowance. Begin sewing 10" (25.5 cm) from the shoulder seam to form an armhole and end at the top of the waistband, leaving an opening for a vent. Turn under the fabric along the vents ¼" (6 mm). Steam-press and stitch to secure.

Step 9: With wrong sides together, join the edges of the turtleneck. Start at the shoulder seam and stitch the sides using a ¼" (6 mm) seam allowance. Stop 4" (10 cm) from the end. Hem the open edges of the turtleneck by folding them under ¼" (.6 cm) on the right side (will be turned under). Steam-press and stitch.

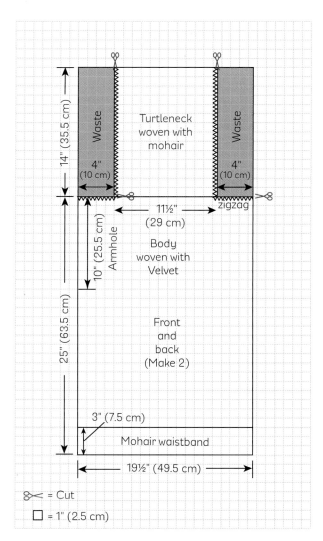

TURTLENECK ASSEMBLY

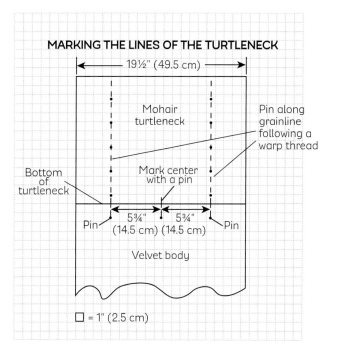

VARIATION

Designed and woven by Sara Goldenberg

We love all the parts of this perky piece woven in a hit-and-miss printed cotton that gives it a hand-dyed look. This is punctuated with dashed double lines of mustard warp floats, making a playful fabric indeed. The stark white knitted trims at neck and waist are unexpected accents that spell fun. Yarns are Universal Yarn Cotton Supreme Splash in Calm Waters and Universal Yarn Nettle Lana in Curry. The trim is Universal Yarn Cotton Supreme in White.

Other fabric ideas

▶ Plaids lend themselves well to straight garment designs. Try this in a plaid with colors similar in value such as deep maroon, midnight blue, and forest green, accented with a spark of aspen gold on the knitted trims.

▶ Changing colors can achieve such different results. Try this garment in the same yarns but in solid white for something that could be dressed up or down.

Alternate styles

▶ Try a vest. Weave short panels and accent with a broad knitted waistband. A deep V-neck gives a new twist to a traditional shape (see top, right).

▶ Create a jumper-style dress by weaving long lengths and topping the neckline off with a soft knitted turtleneck collar.

▶ For a sweater-like interpretation, add sleeves to this basic design with knit cuffs and waistband (see bottom, right).

▶ Try a tweed yarn, using a single yarn in the warp and crossing it with a slightly different color in the weft. Trim with knitting at the neck and waist in a contrasting color.

This easy-to-wear jacket is warm and soft and comfortable. You'll turn to it again and again as a versatile accessory good over corduroys or a wool skirt or most anything, really.

SWEATER JACKET

Designed and woven by *Sara Goldenberg*

This garment requires two warps, one for the body of the jacket and the other for the front trim collar. Brown warpwise accent stripes are broken up by subtle weft float bands for a fabric that is understated yet intriguing.

Body

Garment size: one size fits most.

Garment dimensions: 32" (81.5 cm) from top of shoulder to bottom hem, and 34" (86.5 cm) from side seam to side seam.

Equipment: loom with 20" (51 cm) weaving width, 10-dent reed, 1 shuttle, thread, needles, sewing machine.

Warp yarn: *Interlacements Rick Rack* (100% rayon at 1,200 yd/lb [1,097 m/453 g], 1,200 yd [1097 m] per skein), in Desert Lichen, 575 yd [526 m] or 1 skein needed. *Skacel Kid Paillettes* (42% kid mohair /40% polyester/18% silk at 2,490 yd/lb [2,277 m/453 g], 137 yd/.88 oz [125 m/25 g] per ball) in color #380, Mauve, 430 yd (393 m) or 4 balls needed. *Note: If weaving on a rigid-heddle loom, substitute Kid Seta in Dusty Lilac because the sequins in* the Kid Paillettes get caught in the heddle. *Interlacements Cabled Cotton* (100% mercerized cotton, 1,125 yd/lb [1,029 m/453 g], 270 yd/4 oz [247 m/113 g] per skein) in Fireplace Embers, 155 yd (142 m) or 1 skein needed.

Weft yarn: *Interlacements Rick Rack* (100% rayon at 1,200 yd/lb [1097 m/453 g], 1,200 yd [1097 m] per skein) in Desert Lichen, 830 yd (759 m) or 1 skein needed.

Weave structure: plain weave with weft float accent stripes.

Warp length: 4¾ yd [4.5 m], which includes take-up and 24" (61 cm) loom waste. If weaving on a shaft loom, allow 36" (91.5 cm) for loom waste and increase warp yarn yardage by one third.

Warp width: 20" (51 cm).

Number of warp ends: 197 working ends (242 actual ends).

EPI: 10.

PPI: 8.

PICK-UP STICK PATTERN:

Pick-up pattern: *1 up, 1 down; repeat from *.

Step 1: Up.

Step 2: Pick-up stick.

Step 3: Up.

Step 4: Pick-up stick.

Step 5: Up.

Step 6: Pick-up stick.

Step 7: Up.

Step 8: Weave 9 picks plain weave (starting and ending with a down shed).

Repeat for length of cloth.

SWEATER JACKET DRAFT

bal ⊢— 49x —⊣

	3			3	3	
		2		2		
1		1	1		1	1

plain weave

repeat pattern 8x

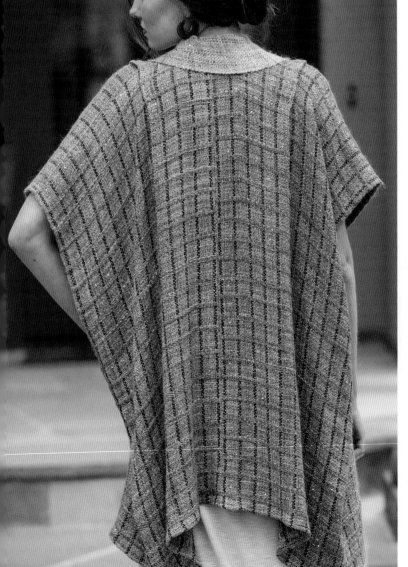

Warp color order:

	bal	Repeat 15 x					
Kp*			2		2		2	90**
rr		3		1		1		3	120
cc	2						2	32
						Total warp ends	242#

Kp = Kid Paillettes, used doubled; rr = Rick Rack; cc = Cabled Cotton*

**90 actual ends; 45 working ends

#242 actual ends; 197 working ends

WEAVING

With Rick Rack, weave 11 picks plain weave and then begin pattern. When you reach the end of the weaving, end with 11 picks plain weave.

FABRIC FINISHING

Secure ends of cloth with overhand knots. Handwash in hot, soapy water and lay flat to dry.

Collar

Dimensions: 78" (198 cm) long plus 1" (2.5 cm) allowance for hems by 5" (12.5 cm) wide (3½" [9 cm] wide on the front).

Warp yarn: *Interlacements Rick Rack* (100% rayon at 1,200 yd/lb [1,097 m/453 g], 1,200 yd per skein [1097 m/453 gr]) in Desert Lichen, 175 yd (160 m) or 1 skein needed.

Weft yarn: *Skacel Kid Paillettes* (42% kid mohair /40% polyester/18% silk at 2,490 yd/lb [2,277 m/453 g], 137 yd/.88 oz [125 m/25 g] per ball), in color #380, Mauve, 112 yd (102.5 m) or 1 ball needed. *Interlacements Rick Rack* (100% rayon, 1,200 yd [1,097 m]) per skein in Desert Lichen, 112 yd (102.5 m) or 1 skein needed. *Note: Kid Paillettes and Rick Rack are used as one.*

Weave structure: plain weave.

Warp length: 3½ yd (3.2 m), which includes take-up and 24" (61 cm) loom waste.

If weaving on a shaft loom, allow 36" (91.5 cm) for loom waste and increase warp yarn yardage by a third.

Warp width: 5" (12.5 cm).

Number of warp ends: 50.

EPI: 10.

PPI: 8.

WEAVING

Wind Kid Paillettes and Rick Rack together on a shuttle. Weave in plain weave until warp runs out.

FABRIC FINISHING

Secure ends of cloth with zigzag stitch and handwash in hot, soapy water. Lay flat to dry.

ASSEMBLY

Step 1: Fold the body fabric in half lengthwise to find the center point.

Step 2: Mark the centerline and secure ½" (1.3 cm) on either side of cutting line with zigzag stitch. Cut cloth in half.

Step 3: With right sides together, stitch up back with a ⅝" (1.5 cm) seam allowance for 32" (81 cm). You may find it helpful to hand baste the cloth before sewing on the machine to ensure that the fabric doesn't slip.

Create neck hole

Step 1: Lay the fabric wrong side down. The neck shaping will start 1" (2.5 cm) down from end of back seam (see template).

Step 2: Before cutting, zigzag stitch around the template and again ½" (1.3 cm) on the inside, as shown in the template.

NECK HOLE

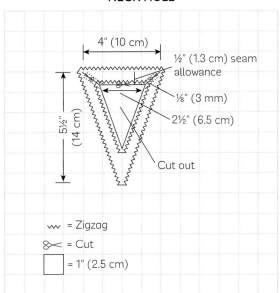

SWEATER JACKET LAYOUT

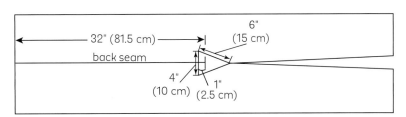

Step 3: Secure with a straight stitch on either side of the snip lines before cutting. Leave ⅛" (3 mm) of uncut cloth at triangle corners.

Step 4: Create a rolled hem around the neckline. A single fold is fine because the collar will cover this.

Step 5: Steam-press hem, hand baste, then secure on the sewing machine.

Side seams

Step 1: Sewing from the bottom up with right sides together, sew side seams with a ⅝" (1.5 cm) seam allowance, leaving 12" (30.5 cm) open for armhole.

Step 2: Make a ½" (1.3 cm) double rolled hem along the bottom edge. Because this hem is so long, it is helpful to hand baste first to keep the hem from shifting.

Attaching the collar/front trim

Step 1: On the wrong side of the fabric, pin the trim with a 1" (2.5 cm) overlap along the inside edge of the jacket front. Later, the collar will be folded over the edge to the front.

Step 2: Hand baste the trim into place, starting from the center back and working down. *Note: Stop basting 2" (5 cm) from the bottom on both sides so you can adjust the trim lengths after stitching the collar. Begin sewing at the center back, stitching down each side of the trim and stopping 2" (5 cm) before the bottom on both sides.*

Step 3: On ends of the trims, create a rolled hem. Zigzag stitch and if necessary, cut off any excess; then pin and hand baste, lining up the bottom of the trim with the bottom of the jacket.

Step 4: After the bottom of the trim is sewn into place, fold the trim piece over the edge to the front and pin,

baste, and stitch. The trim piece will measure 3½" (9 cm) wide on the front. Hand tack the edge of the trim to the ground cloth so that it lies flat.

Shoulder pleat

Step 1: Make a pleat at the shoulder by folding the fabric under ¾" (2 cm) 11½" (29 cm) from the outside edge along the top of the shoulder. The fold should measure 6" (15 cm): 3" (7.5 cm) in the front and 3" (7.5 cm) in the back measuring from the top of the shoulder.

Step 2: Stitch by hand with a backstitch (see page 12 for how-to). Alternately, you could machine sew with a long stitch, hand basting first.

Other fabric ideas

▶ Medium-weight yarns work well for this design, and using novelty yarns as accents works to make a stunning fabric, as we've done here. Try using the same yarns in a different colorway, such as a mix of blues and greens.

▶ Plain weave has such possibilities and should never be underestimated—especially with so many high-quality yarns available. An idea worth exploring is to look at yarns dyed by indie dyers who often dye different yarns in the same colorway. Combining a variety of yarns in the same color would create a garment rich in color and texture.

▶ If you're a handspinner, think about spinning up a dyed merino batt. Ply it and use it for warp or alternate handspun with a tweedy commercial yarn for a homespun feel. Weave with a handspun or commercially made singles yarn for weft.

Alternate styles

▶ By weaving 2 short panels, you can create a vestlike top. A V-neck trimmed in a contrasting texture is the only accent (see top, right).

▶ Just by weaving longer lengths, you can create a coatlike look. Try contrasting trims around the neck, front opening, and bottom edge.

▶ Shaping the neck changes the look of this simple garment shape. A decorative bottom border could be highly patterned for ethnic styling (see bottom, right).

If you've never tried weaving with ribbon, this stunning T-top is a great place to begin. Three ribbons are used: two different colorways of a sparkly space-dyed ribbon alternated with another space-dyed ribbon with blocks of gold squares. The result gives the piece an overall hit-and-miss look that makes for a dressed-up top. All of the ribbon yarns are threaded in the slots and alternate with a fine wool-blend yarn.

RIBBON T-TOP

Designed and woven by *Sara Goldenberg*

Like most of the designs in this book, rectangles are used to create a simple garment (three rectangles in this case). The stripes, formed by alternating wool and ribbon in the warp, are used vertically for the body of the top and turned for horizontal stripes in the bodice/sleeve piece. Vents are left at the sides. Additionally, the sleeve seams are left unsewn for an open look.

Garment size: medium.

Finished dimensions: 28" (71 cm) from top of shoulder to bottom of body, 23½" (59.5 cm) from side seam to side seam, 31" (79 cm) from sleeve end to sleeve end.

Equipment: loom with at least 25" (63. 5 cm) weaving width, 8-dent reed, 1 shuttle, sewing machine.

Warp yarn: *Prism Yarn Galaxy,* hand-dyed ribbon (95% nylon/5% metallic polyester at 432 yd/lb [395 m/453 g], 54 yd/2 oz [49.5 m/57 g] per skein) in Sierra, 162 yd (148 m) or 3 skeins needed. *Prism Yarn Constellation,* hand-dyed ribbon (95% nylon/5% metallic polyester at 432 yd/ lb [395 m/453 g], 54 yd/2 oz [49.5 m/57 g] per skein) in color Twilight, 82 yd (75 m) or 2 skeins needed. *Prism Yarn Constellation Layers,* hand-dyed ribbon (95% nylon/5% metallic polyester at 432 yd/lb [395 m/453 g], 54 yd/2 oz [49.5 m/57 g] per skein) in color Bracken, 78 yd (71 m) or 2 skeins needed. *Prism Yarn Petite Madison Layers,* hand-dyed yarn (75% merino wool/15% cashmere/10% silk at 1,690 yd/lb [1,545 m/453 g], 372 yd/3.5 oz [340 m/100 g] per skein) in color Platinum, 325 yd (297 m) or 1 skein needed.

Weft yarn: *Prism Yarn Petite Madison Layers,* hand-dyed yarn (75% merino wool/15% cashmere/10% silk at 1,690 yd/lb [1,545 m/453 g], 372 yd/3.5 oz [340 m/100 g] per skein) in color Platinum, 500 yd (457 m) or 2 skeins needed.

Weave structure: plain weave.

Warp length: 3¼ yd (3 m), which includes take-up and 24" (61 cm) loom waste. If weaving on a shaft loom, allow 36" (91.5 cm) for loom waste and increase warp yarn yardage by a third.

Warp width: just under 25" (63.5 cm).

Number of warp ends: 199.

EPI: 8.

PPI: 7.

Warp color order:

	Repeat 25x		Repeat 24x		end		
PML*	1+		1	1	1	1	1	100
Galaxy		1		1		1	50
Con**			1				25
Con L***					1		24
					Total warp ends		199

PML = Petite Madison Layers, Platinum

**Con = Constellation, Twilight*

***Con L = Constellation Layers, Bracken*

+ = start threading in a hole. All Petite Madison Layers will be threaded in the holes.

Warping note: Because the ribbon yarn is bulky, we suggest winding the warp on a warping board. Wind each warp yarn separately and then sley them following the warp color order.

WEAVING

Weave with Petite Madison in Platinum until warp runs out. Beat gently at 7 ppi. The selvedges will be exposed in the final piece. Adjust your weaver's angle so that your selvedges have a firm and even edge.

FABRIC FINISHING

Secure ends with overhand knots. Wash in warm, soapy water by hand and lay flat to dry.

ASSEMBLY

Step 1: Zigzag stitch the ends of the fabric and cut off the fringe. Because this fabric is a fairly loose weave, it's important to zigzag stitch between panels before cutting apart.

Step 2: Create 3 panels: 1 at 33" (84 cm) and 2 at 20" (51 cm). The top panel (33" [84 cm]) forms the bodice and sleeves or yoke. The other 2 panels form the body.

Step 3: Make ½" (1.3 cm) double rolled hems at either end of the top yoke panel, yielding an overall finished length of 31" (78.5 cm). Use a long stitch length and machine stitch slowly to avoid snagging the ribbon. Steam-press using a press cloth with firm pressure. Pin all of the hems before stitching. Topstitch on the right side as close to the edge as possible.

Step 4: Make ½" (1.3 cm) double rolled hems at the bottom edge of the front and back panels of the body for a total final length of 16.5" (42 cm).

Step 5: At the top of the front and back panels, make a single ½" (1.3 cm) fold on the right side of the fabric (facing the opposite direction of bottom hem). *Note: The yoke will cover this hem.*

Step 6: Cut out a 6" × 7" (15 × 18 cm) template for the neck opening. Offset the neck hole so that it is down 1" (2.5 cm) farther in the front than in the back. Center the template from the ends of both sleeves (see diagram on page 112). Before making hems, reinforce all corners of the neck opening with two lines of straight stitching. Fold under all sides of the neck opening for a double rolled hem. Steam-press with a press cloth, pin, and then machine stitch into place.

Step 7: Find and mark the center of the yoke. Overlap

the sleeve panel ½" (1.3 cm) on top of the front panel so that the single rolled hem is covered by the sleeve panel.

Step 8: Pin from the center out, hand baste, and machine stitch. Leave ⅝" (1.5 cm) unsewn at either edge. This will be used for seam allowance on the side seams. Stitch as close to the edge as possible.

Step 9: Repeat with the back panel making sure the front and back panels line up with one another. Hand tack the edge of the seam overlap from the front and back panels to the yoke panel.

Step 10: With right sides together, sew side seams with a ⅝" (1.5 cm) seam allowance. Begin from the top, stopping 3" (7.5 cm) from the bottom edge to make a side vent. Fold back the vent fabric ⅝" (1.5 cm) and tack in place by hand. Steam-press the seams open.

NECK HOLE

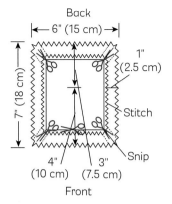

Back

← 6" (15 cm) →

7" (18 cm)

1" (2.5 cm)

Stitch

4" (10 cm) 3" (7.5 cm) Snip

Front

✂ = Cut

------ = Straight stitch

〰〰〰 = Zigzag stitch

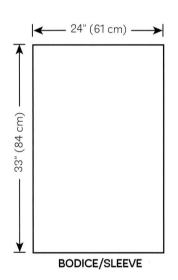

← 24" (61 cm) →

33" (84 cm)

BODICE/SLEEVE

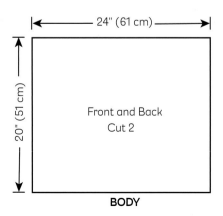

← 24" (61 cm) →

20" (51 cm)

Front and Back
Cut 2

BODY

VARIATION

Designed and woven by Sara Goldenberg
Broad stripes in two different variegated yarns create movement and visual interest. Solid gold warp stripes lend contrast to this fabric that is tied together with a neutral beige yarn, letting the warp yarns speak for themselves. The stripes are threaded in the warp and used vertically in the body and then turned in the bodice/sleeves for horizontal stripes. Warp yarns are Skacel Austermann Murano Lace in gray, color 4, and blue-purple, color 8, and Brown Sheep Nature Spun, sportweight in Sunburst Gold. The weft is Alpaca Fiber Cooperative of North America, #921, 2/70's in Fawn.

simple woven garments

Other fabric ideas

▸ Use a variegated or spaced-dyed yarn for narrow stripes on a solid ground. For a medium-weight garment, weave in a sportweight wool.

▸ On the same warp, weave the bodice/sleeve piece with textured knots or loops and the body of the garment in plain weave.

▸ Combine stripes and plaids. Thread up a striped warp; weave the body of the fabric in one color and cross the warp as threaded for the body/sleeves.

Alternate styles

▸ Weave short front and back panels as well as the bodice/sleeve piece and add knitted trim at the sleeves and bottom edge (see top right).

▸ Weave elbow-length sleeves and give the top an ethnic look with tufts of ghiordes knots (see page 125). Leave the bottom plain with side vents (see bottom, right).

▸ By weaving longer panels for the front and back, you can create a dress or long tunic. Adding trim between the bodice and the body gives the piece an Empire waist.

This sporty top is a study in stripes—fun to weave because they are ever changing. The stripes are woven in the weft, which means you can vary them at will versus threading them in the warp where they are fixed. The back is a solid color. We love the detail along the sleeves where the striped front meets the solid-colored back.

HOODIE

Designed and woven by *Sara Goldenberg*

Stripes are woven in the weft and turned for vertical stripes in the sweater. As a weaver, you can have fun creating nonrepeating stripes. Here, they modulate from sleeve to sleeve on the front of the sweater. The back side is left plain. Yardage waste is eliminated by using the sleeve cutouts to make the hood!

Garment size: small.

Finished dimensions: 64" (162.5 cm) sleeve to sleeve, 21" (53.5 cm) from neckline to bottom of knitted trim.

A note about sizing: To determine the correct size for you, measure your wingspan from wrist to wrist and then add 10% for take-up and shrinkage. Likewise, measure from your shoulder to your waist and add 5% for draw-in to determine the width of your warp.

Equipment: loom with 20" (51 cm) weaving width, 8-dent reed, 2 to 4 shuttles, size 10 double-pointed knitting needles, 29" (73.5 cm) size 10 circular knitting needle, size J crochet hook.

Gauge: cuffs—21 rows and 17 stitches in 4" (10 cm). Waist Band—21 rows and 13 stitches in 4" (10 cm).

Warp yarn: *Berroco Blackstone Tweed* (65% wool/25% mohair/10% angora at 1,188 yd/lb [1,086 m/453 g] 130 yd/1.75 oz [119 m/50 g] per ball) in color #2603, Ancient Mariner, 800 yd (732 m) or 7 skeins needed.

Weft yarn: *Berroco Blackstone Tweed* (65% wool/25% mohair/10% angora at 1,188 yd/ lb [1,086m/453 g], 130 yd/1.75 oz [119 m/50 g] per ball) in color #2603, Ancient Mariner, 45 yd (41 m) or 1 skein needed; and color #2663, Marsh, 335 yd (306 m) or 3 skeins needed. *Berroco Ultra Alpaca* (50% alpaca/50% wool at 983 yd/lb [898 m/453 g], 215 yd/3.5 oz [198 m/100 g] per skein) in color #6211, Duncan, 92 yd (84 m) or 1 skein needed. *Berroco Ultra Alpaca Light* (50% alpaca/50% wool at 1,316 yd/lb [1,203 m/453 g], 144 yd/1.75 oz [133 m/50 g] per skein) in color #4294, Turquoise Mix, 22 yd (20 m) or 1 skein needed; and color #4275, Pea Soup Mix, 73 yd (67 m) or 1 skein needed.

Knitted trim: *Berroco Ultra Alpaca* (50% alpaca/50% wool at 983 yd/lb [898 m/453 g], 215 yd/3.5 oz [198 m/100 g] per skein) in color #6211, Duncan, 102 yd (93.5 m) or 1 skein needed.

Weave structure: plain weave.

Warp length: 5 yd (4.5 m), which includes take-up and 24" (61 cm) loom waste. If weaving on a shaft loom, allow 36" (91.5 cm) for loom waste and increase warp yarn yardage by a third.

Warp width: 20" (51 cm).

Number of warp ends: 160.

EPI: 8.

PPI: 7.

WEAVING

Back panel

Weave in plain weave with Blackstone Tweed Marsh until panel measures 68" (173 cm) without tension. Weave a 2" (5 cm) spacer with scrap yarn and begin the front panel.

Front panel

Wind shuttles with Ancient Mariner, Duncan, Turquoise, and Pea Soup. The pattern below has many color shifts; feel free to explore and create your own striped pattern.

Left sleeve

Step 1: Alternate 2 picks Duncan and 2 picks Turquoise; repeat 5 times.

Step 2: Alternate 3 picks Pea Soup and 2 picks Turquoise; repeat 2 times, ending with 3 picks Pea Soup.

Step 3: Alternate 1 pick Ancient Mariner and 1 pick Pea Soup; repeat 4 times.

Step 4: Alternate 1 pick Ancient Mariner and 1 pick Turquoise; repeat 4 times and end with 1 pick Turquoise.

Step 5: Alternate 3 picks Duncan and 2 picks Turquoise; repeat 3 times.

Step 6: Alternate 3 picks Duncan and 2 picks Pea Soup; repeat 3 times.

Step 7: Alternate 2 picks Turquoise and 2 picks Pea Soup; repeat 2 times.

Step 8: 5 picks Ancient Mariner.

Step 9: Alternate 1 pick Duncan and 1 pick Ancient Mariner; repeat 5 times.

Step 10: 4 picks Ancient Mariner.

Step 11: Alternate 3 picks Turquoise and 1 pick Duncan; repeat 3 times.

Step 12: Alternate 3 picks Pea Soup and 1 pick Duncan; repeat 3 times.

Step 13: Alternate 3 picks Turquoise and 1 pick Duncan; repeat 3 times.

Step 14: 4 picks Duncan.

Front (center)

Step 1: 8 picks Duncan.

Step 2: Alternate 1 pick Ancient Mariner and 1 pick Duncan; repeat 6 times.

Step 3: 10 picks Ancient Mariner.

Step 4: 3 picks Pea Soup.

Step 5: Alternate 1 pick Ancient Mariner and 1 pick Pea Soup; repeat 6 times.

Step 6: 2 picks Pea Soup.

Step 7: 12 picks Turquoise.

Step 8: Alternate 2 picks Duncan and 2 picks Turquoise; repeat 3 times.

Step 9: 2 picks Turquoise.

Step 10: Alternate 1 pick Turquoise and 1 pick Ancient Mariner; repeat 5 times.

Step 11: Alternate 1 pick Duncan and 2 picks Ancient Mariner; repeat 5 times.

Step 12: 8 picks Ancient Mariner.

Step 13: Alternate 2 picks Pea Soup and 1 pick Ancient Mariner; repeat 3 times.

Step 14: 12 picks Pea Soup.

Step 15: 12 picks Turquoise.

Step 16: 6 picks Duncan.

Step 17: 4 picks Ancient Mariner.

Step 18: 8 picks Pea Soup.

Step 19: 8 picks Turquoise.

Step 20: 13 picks Duncan.

Right sleeve

Step 1: Alternate 3 picks Pea Soup and 1 pick Duncan; repeat 3 times.

Step 2: Alternate 3 picks Turquoise and 1 pick Duncan; repeat 3 times.

Step 3: Repeat Steps 1 and 2 three more times.

Step 4: Alternate 3 picks Pea Soup and 2 picks Duncan; repeat 3 times.

Step 5: Alternate 3 picks Turquoise and 2 picks Duncan; repeat 3 times.

Step 6: Alternate 2 picks Pea Soup and 2 picks Duncan; repeat 3 times.

Step 7: Alternate 2 picks Turquoise and 2 picks Duncan; repeat 3 times.

Step 8: 5 picks Duncan.

Note: If your weaving comes up short after weaving the above, weave a little longer so that your front and back pieces match. You want both the front and the back to measure 68" (173 cm).

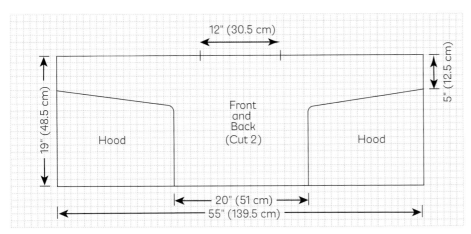

HOODIE LAYOUT AND CUTTING GUIDE

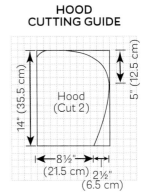

HOOD CUTTING GUIDE

FABRIC FINISHING

Secure the ends of fabric with overhand knots. Wash by hand in hot, soapy water, rinse, and lay flat to dry.

ASSEMBLY

Step 1: Separate the front and back. Machine zigzag on either side of the front and back panels (on either side of scrap yarn) before cutting apart.

Step 2: Stack the panels right sides together; mark the center point of each piece.

Step 3: Make a template for the sleeves and mark the fabric (see illustration on page 117). Zigzag stitch around the outside of the template before cutting. Mark a 12" wide (31.5 cm) neck hole (see illustration).

Step 4: Machine stitch the shoulder and top sleeve seam with a ¼" (6 mm) seam allowance. Be sure not to stitch together the neck-hole area. Work from the edge of the neck hole to the end of the sleeve.

Step 5: Sew sides and bottom of sleeves with a ¼" (6 mm) seam allowance.

Step 6: Cut away excess cloth (this waste will be used for the hood) leaving ¼" (6 mm) seam allowance beyond the zigzag stitch.

Knit the cuffs

Step 1: Using Ultra Alpaca in Duncan, pick up stitches every 2 warp threads using a size J crochet hook. Pull yarn from the inside out, pulling a few stitches at a time. Then transfer to size 10 double-pointed needles as you go, 11 stitches per needle, 4 needles total.

You will have roughly 44 stitches (you want to have a number divisible by 4 to create the rib).

Step 2: Join the yarn and k2, p2 all the way around to create a ribbed cuffed; continue in pattern for 15 rows.

Step 3: Cast off in pattern.

Step 4: Repeat for other cuff.

Knit the waistband

Step 1: Pick up 150 stitches using the crochet hook and transfer to a 29" (73.5 cm) size 10 circular needle.

Step 2: Join the yarn and knit 7, purl 3.

Step 3: Continue in pattern until the band measures 6" (15 cm).

Step 4: Cast off in pattern.

Make the hood and shape the neckline:

Step 1: Cut hood pieces according to diagram on page 117. Check the pieces against the neck hole, and allowing for ⅜" (1 cm) seam allowances, be sure that it fits the space.

Step 2: With right sides together, stitch the pieces together using a ⅜" (1 cm) seam allowance.

Step 3: Hem the front of the hood by turning it under 1" (2.5 cm) and stitching.

Step 4: Place the right side of the hood to the inside of the back and stitch in place using a ⅜" (1 cm) seam allowance.

Step 5: Shape the front of the neck opening by folding it under ¼" (6 mm) and handstitching.

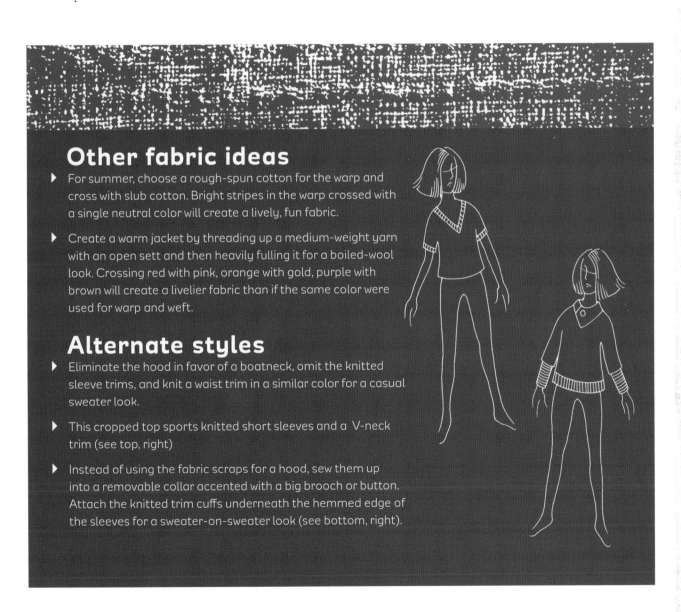

Other fabric ideas

▸ For summer, choose a rough-spun cotton for the warp and cross with slub cotton. Bright stripes in the warp crossed with a single neutral color will create a lively, fun fabric.

▸ Create a warm jacket by threading up a medium-weight yarn with an open sett and then heavily fulling it for a boiled-wool look. Crossing red with pink, orange with gold, purple with brown will create a livelier fabric than if the same color were used for warp and weft.

Alternate styles

▸ Eliminate the hood in favor of a boatneck, omit the knitted sleeve trims, and knit a waist trim in a similar color for a casual sweater look.

▸ This cropped top sports knitted short sleeves and a V-neck trim (see top, right)

▸ Instead of using the fabric scraps for a hood, sew them up into a removable collar accented with a big brooch or button. Attach the knitted trim cuffs underneath the hemmed edge of the sleeves for a sweater-on-sweater look (see bottom, right).

If you've ever examined the fabric of a Chanel jacket, you can see where we channeled our inspiration for this stunning interpretation. The accent trims are the perfect opportunity to practice your finger-controlled techniques. A hand-braided trim outlines either side of the fringy front edges.

ODE TO COCO

Fabric designed by *Jane Patrick*; garment designed and sewn by *Sara Goldenberg*; woven by *Betty Paepke*

Yarns such as the ones we've used here create a fabric that is rich in color and texture. Honey-colored yarns are used in the warp. For weft, we switched out one honey-colored yarn for a gray to add more depth to the fabric. Additionally, we separated the blocks of this log-cabin fabric with a variegated yarn that also changes in texture along its length.

We wove the trims on the same warp using different weaving techniques. The trim strips were sewn to the bottom of the jacket and the ends of the sleeves. We used ghiordes knots for the fringes and rows of soumak for a braided look. The body of the fabric is log cabin with two threads outlining each block (see page 127 for information on log cabin). Because our colors are close together, the changes are subtle.

Garment size: medium.

Finished dimensions: 24" (61 cm) from top of shoulder to bottom edge, 22" (56 cm) from side seam to side seam, 27½" (70 cm) from edge of neck hole to end of sleeve.

Equipment: loom with 25" (63.5 cm) weaving width, 10-dent reed, 3 shuttles (more if you have them would be handy), sewing machine.

Warp yarn: *Trendsetter Twiggy* (47% linen/32% viscose/21% polyamide at 773 yd/lb [707 m/453 g], 85 yd/1.75 oz [78 m/50 g] per skein) in color #103, Cream Puff, 525 yd (480 m) or 7 skeins needed. *Trendsetter Zoe* (50% cotton/45% viscose/5% polyester at

682 yd/lb [624 m/453 g], 75 yd/1.75 oz [68.5 m/50 g] per skein) in #50 Apple Pie, 525 yd (480 m) or 7 skeins needed. *Trendsetter Summit* (44% wool/44% acrylic/12% nylon at 1,006/ yd/lb [920 m/453 g], 110 yd/1.75 oz [100.5 m/50 g] per ball) in color #4202 Pottery Barn, 200 yd (183 m) or 2 balls needed.

Weft yarn: *Trendsetter Twiggy* (47% linen/32% viscose/21% polyamide at 773 yd/lb [707 m/453 g], 85 yd/1.75 oz [78 m/50 g] per skein) in color #92, Mushroom Soup, 275 yd (251.5 m) or 4 skeins needed. *Trendsetter Zoe* (50% cotton/45% viscose/5% polyester at 682 yd/lb [624 m/453 g], 75yd/1.75 oz

[68.5 m/50 g] per skein) in #50 Apple Pie, 275 yd (251.5 m) or 4 skeins needed. *Trendsetter Summit* (44% wool/44% acrylic/12% nylon at 1,006 yd/lb [920 m/453 g], 110 yd/1.75 oz [100.5 m/50 g] per ball) in color #4202 Pottery Barn, 185 yd (169 m) or 2 balls needed. *Trendsetter Dune* in (45% mohair/25% acrylic/20% viscose/6% wool/4% polyester at 791 yd/lb [79.5 m/453 g], 87 yd/1.75 oz [79.5 m/50 g] per ball) in color #124 Mink Blush, 50 yd (46 mm) or 1 ball needed. *Trendsetter Luna* (100% polyester at 6,588 yd/lb [6,024 m/453 g], 350 yd/.85 oz [329 m/25 g] per ball) in color #100, Gold, 20 yd (19 m) or 1 ball needed. *Trendsetter Merino 8*

(100% merino at 915 yd/lb [837 m/453 g], 100 yd/1.75 oz [91.5 m/50 g] per ball) in Merino 8 Shadow color #126, 31 yd (29 m) or 1 ball needed.

Weave structure: plain weave woven in log cabin with accents of ghiordes knots (see page 125) and soumak (see page 123).

Warp length: 5 yd (4.5 m), which includes take-up and 24" (61 cm) for loom waste. If weaving on a shaft loom, allow 36" (91.5 cm) for loom waste and increase warp yarn yardage by one third.

Warp width: 25" (63.5).

Number of warp ends: 250.

EPI: 10.

PPI: 8.

Warp color order:

	Repeat 10 times					end		
	5 x			5x		5x		
Zoe*	1				1	1		105
Twiggy**		1		1			1	105
Summit			2		2			40
						Total ends		250

Colors: *Apple Pie **Cream Puff

WEAVING

Weave fabric as threaded but substitute Twiggy in Mushroom Soup for the Twiggy Cream Puff. Weave pattern for body of fabric until it measures 120" (305 cm). Weave trims as instructed.

Body of garment

Step 1: Alternate Zoe in Apple Pie and Twiggy in Mushroom Soup 5 times.

Step 2: Weave 2 rows of Summit.

Step 3: Alternate Twiggy in Mushroom Soup and Zoe in Apple Pie 5 times.

Step 4: Weave 2 rows of Summit.

Step 5: Repeat Steps 1–4 until weaving measures 120" (305 cm).

Cuffs and bottom trim

Step 1: On a closed shed, work a row of ghiordes knots (see page 125) using Dune. The length of the knots should be about 1½" (3.8 cm). You'll trim these after washing.

Step 2: Alternate Shadow and Luna 12 times or for 2" (5 cm). End with Shadow.

Step 3: Wind Zoe Apple Pie and Twiggy Cream Puff together on a short shuttle. Work all the way across the warp with 3 × 3 soumak (see page 123).

Step 4: Weave 1 pick of Shadow.

Step 5: Work a row of 3 × 3 soumak back to the other selvedge.

Step 6: Weave 6 rows with Shadow.

Step 7: Repeat Steps 3–5.

Step 8: Alternate Zoe Apple Pie and Twiggy Mushroom Soup 8 times or for 2" (5 cm).

Step 9: Repeat Steps 1–8 two more times.

FABRIC FINISHING

Because this piece is so large, cut the body of the garment into 2 equal pieces. Fold the plain-weave section in half lengthwise and mark. Zigzag stitch on either side of the cutting line before cutting apart. Also zigzag between the body fabric and trim pieces and remove all of the trim before washing. Handwash all pieces in warm water and mild soap. Lay flat to dry and give the fabric a good steam-press using a press cloth.

ASSEMBLY

Step 1: Zigzag stitch 1½" (3.8 cm) on either side of the center of the front panel. These stitch lines will secure the opening of the jacket that will be cut later.

Step 2: Stack the 2 panels on top of each other, right sides together.

Step 3: On the top edge, find the center of the panels. Measure and mark out 4" (10 cm) on either side of the center. This will form the 8" (20.5 cm) neck opening. From these marks, pin the panels together along the top edge, excluding neck-hole area. Starting at the

SOUMAK

Soumak is a rug technique that can also be used on a balanced weave to add texture. You could describe soumak as a looping technique, similar to Brooks bouquet in process. In the case of soumak, however, you are completely covering the warp instead of creating a lacy, or open, effect as in Brooks bouquet.

Soumak sits on top of the surface. When working from one selvedge and back again, a knitted appearance is achieved. Because soumak does not provide structural stability, use it in conjunction with a plain-weave ground. Work soumak on a closed shed. Though there are numerous ways to work soumak, we present only regular soumak here.

Soumak has a directional angle. When you work right to left in regular soumak, you'll see that the wrapping leans to the right. On the return trip, the wraps lean to the left. When these 2 rows are beaten close together, the fabric looks knitted.

3 over 3 Regular Soumak

Step 1: Wind a butterfly or use a small shuttle with pattern yarn. Insert the tail of the pattern weft under the selvedge thread and then over, under, over the next 3 warps, pulling the tail to the back of the weaving (**Figure 1**).

Step 2: On a closed shed, working right to left, travel over 3 warps right to left and wrap around those threads left to right (**Figure 2**).

Step 3: Bring the thread to the surface and travel over 6 warps (the first 3 you just encircled plus the next 3). Travel back 3 warps to the right and encircle these right to left (**Figure 3**); repeat this step until you reach the other selvedge.

Step 4: Weave 1 row of plain weave (**Figure 4**).

Step 5: To travel up to the next row, insert your butterfly in between the last 2 or 3 warps and bring it out at the side (**Figure 5**).

Step 6: Work in the opposite direction as for the first row in 3 over 3 soumak (**Figures 6 and 7**).

Figure 1

Figure 2

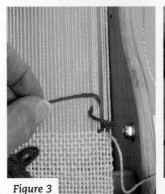

Figure 3

Figure 4

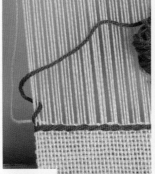

Figure 5

Figure 6

Figure 7

outside edge of the shoulder/sleeve, stitch with a ½" (1.3 cm) seam allowance tapering to ⅛" (3 mm) seam allowance at the neck-hole opening (see template).

Step 4: To create sleeves and side seams, make a template (see template). You will use the template on one side and then flip it for the other. On the first side, pin template to stacked panels, right sides together. Zigzag stitch around the template. Cut away excess cloth, leaving ¼" (6 mm) seam allowance around the edges. Repeat on other side. Sew bottom of sleeve/side seams.

Step 5: Turn garment right side out.

Step 6: Cut down the center of the front between the zigzag stitching done in Step 1 and then pull out the yarn to the zigzag stitching for fringe on either side of the jacket opening.

Step 7: Separate trim pieces. Straight-stitch along the edge of the soumak and zigzag stitch ½" (1.3 cm) below the row of ghiordes knots. (The straight stitch is less visible along the soumak edge; zigzag stitch is better for the fringe areas.) Ravel the edge along the zigzag stitching for a 1" (2.5 cm) fringe. The ground fabric fringe will peek out below the row of ghiordes knots.

Attach the cuffs

Step 1: Starting at the underarm seam, attach the cuff with pins beginning at the selvedge edge of the trim fabric. Stitch by hand at top edge of cuff and then

stitch a second row using a backstitch down the center of the soumak. Leave 1½" (3.8 cm) of cuff unattached to arm fabric to determine amount needed to go around the wrist. You may need to cut off excess.

Step 2: Secure the ends of the trim band with zigzag stitching before cutting; leave enough length so that the cut edge can overlap the selvedge edge by ½" (1.3 cm).

Step 3: Stitch remainder of the cuff into place and then stitch up the opening of the cuff.

Step 4: Repeat for second cuff.

Attach the waist trim

Step 1: Use the remaining portions of trim fabric from the cuffs for the front waistband area; use the third section of trim for the back.

Step 2: Find the center of the back of the jacket and the center of the back waist trim panel.

Step 3: Begin pinning back panel from the center out so that the ghiordes knots hit right at the bottom edge of the jacket.

Step 4: Pin both sides of back panel and then pin the front portions of the waistband into place. Overlap sections by ⅛" (.5 cm).

Step 5: The front waist panel should end 1½" (3.8 cm) before the edge of the woven portion of the front panel

SLEEVE SIDE SEAM TEMPLATE

⅛" (3 mm)
28¾" (73 cm)
½" (1.3 cm) seam allowance
stitching stops 4" from centerline
4"
6½" (16.5 cm)
Center 22½" (57 cm)
13" (33 cm)
□ = 1" (2.5 cm)
11½" (29 cm)

FRONT LAPELS AND NECKLINE

Fold under ¼" (6 mm)
Braided trim
2½" (6.5 cm)
Trim
Fringe
Fringe
Trim
Trim
Trim
½" (1.3 cm)
Stitching ¼" (6 cm)

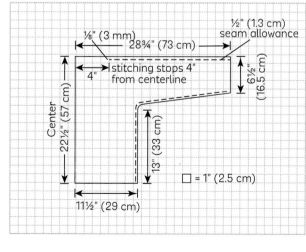

GHIORDES KNOT

The ghiordes knot is probably the most-used knot for pile rugs because it is a highly secure knot—one that doesn't ravel or come undone. It is also quite versatile in that you can tie knots from either a continuous strand or from cut pieces. Ghiordes knots also offer design freedom in that every knot can be a different color.

Generally, pile is used for thick rugs. Individual knots are worked across the warp and 2 or more rows of plain weave are woven between rows of knots to create a stable fabric. Here, we've used single rows of ghiordes knots for an accent on a balanced-weave fabric.

Making a ghiordes knot with a continuous length of yarn

Step 1: Weave a background base of plain weave. Wind a butterfly of yarn from a length of yarn or use the yarn right out of the ball.

Step 2: To tie a knot, working from the right, bring the working end of your yarn down through a pair of warps. The working end is under the right warp (**Figure 1**).

Step 3: Bring the working end over the top of this pair, right to left (**Figure 2**).

Step 4: Finish by bringing the working end (left to right) up through the center (**Figure 3**). *Note: Both of the ends are in between 2 warp threads.*

Step 5: Pull the ends down to the woven web and snug up the knot (**Figure 4**).

Step 6: Cut off the working end (**Figure 5**). Move onto the next warp pair and repeat Steps 2–5 for the next knot. Continue across the warp. After you've completed a row of knots, weave plain weave. Trim your knots to uniform lengths after the weaving has been washed.

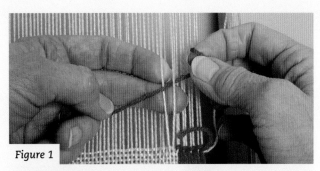

Figure 1

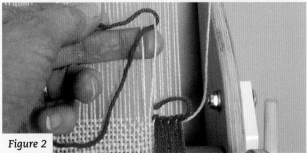

Figure 2

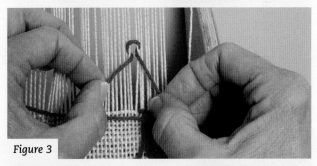

Figure 3

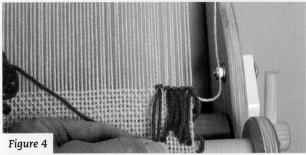

Figure 4

Figure 5

Ode to Coco

(does not include fringe area). Pin front waist panels into place. Cut off any excess (be sure to zigzag stitch before trimming).

Step 6: Hand tack the waist trim to the jacket. Machine stitch into place down the center of the top braid. Then using an overcast stitch, handsew the front trim to back trim on both sides.

Shape and finish the collar and front opening

Step 1: Fold the cloth down ¼" (6 mm) at back edge of neckline. Press and machine stitch into place. Fold the collar/front open. The top edge of collar/front measures 2½" (6.5 cm) at the top and tapers to ½" (1.3 cm) at the bottom edge. Steam-press and pin into

place so both sides are even. Machine straight stitch ¼" (6 mm) from the outside edge (see illustration on page 124).

Step 2: Trim ghiordes knots to 1" (2.5 cm) on cuffs and waist trim. The jacket fringe will hang down about ½" (1.3 cm) below ghiordes knots.

Step 3: Make the braided trim for the collar/front: Using 3 strands of pink merino 8 Shadow, make two 25" (63.5 cm) long braids. Allow extra yarn to tie knots at the beginning and end of the braids. Handstitch the braid down the front along the fringe line ¼" (6 mm) from the edge. Start and end the braids with a tight knot, lining the knots up with the top and bottom edges.

Other fabric ideas

▸ Use a fine wool/silk-blend yarn sett at 12 ends per inch and heavily full it for a thick fabric with shiny flecks. Because the wool will shrink and the silk will not, the finished fabric will have a most appealing bumpy surface.

▸ Use a wool crepe yarn closely sett for a fabric that has bounce and stretch.

▸ Dive into your stash and choose yarns close in color but with varied textures. Thread these at random in the reed and tie it all together with a smooth yarn in a similar color.

Alternate styles

▸ Instead of long sleeves, create a short-sleeved jacket with button accents down the middle. Add a front band for accent (see top, right).

▸ Go casual with a plaid fabric for a slipover accented with fringe and a front tassel.

▸ A tailored look is achieved with little patch pockets and a simple collar (see bottom, right).

LOG CABIN

Log cabin is a specific kind of color-and-weave effect, which is a pattern created in weaving by the interaction of color in the woven web. Generally, log cabin involves 2 colors of yarn, sometimes of two sizes. Log cabin appears to be an intricate structure, but it's just over-and-under plain weave. The structure never changes. What changes is how the colors are woven.

Why does this work? If you examine the fabric, you can see that a color is either on top of the surface or underneath it. When a white weft, for example, crosses a black warp, the white will show on the top (and black on the bottom). When a color is repeated, it alters how the color appears in the weaving (whether it is seen or not seen), creating its distinct pattern. This is what shifts the pattern in log cabin.

I like to think of log cabin as a block weave where block A is threaded dark, light, dark, light, etc., and block B is threaded light, dark, light, dark, etc. To get the colors to shift, a color is repeated at the edge of the blocks. For example, thread block A: dark, light, dark, light, dark, light and then thread block B; light, dark, light, dark, light, dark. Notice that at the transition between blocks A and B, 2 light ,warps are threaded next to each other. This same sequence is repeated in the weft and creates a weave-on-weave look.

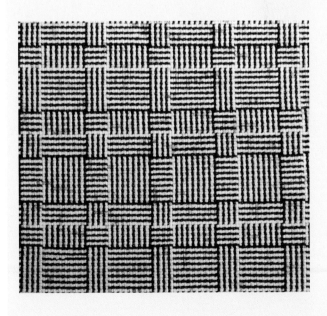

Our peplum is just the thing to wear when it's blistering hot. A hint of handpainted ribbon yarn adds a playful touch to the textured white-on-white fabric. The yarn is a soft, soft bamboo, making a fabric with exquisite drape that is comfy to wear.

PEPLUM

Designed by *Jane Patrick and Sara Goldenberg*; woven by *David Pipinich*

This summery design is made up of different woven interlacements that work together to make a most weaverly top indeed. Here's where you discover the power a pick-up stick wields on a rigid-heddle loom—making three distinct interlacements—all on one warp (a draft for shaft looms is also provided). The zigzag motif on the front is on-loom embroidery, lending a bit of color and enhancing the pattern-on-pattern look.

Garment size: small.

Note: This garment is more fitted that the others in the book, and if you don't do a muslin pattern for any other project, this is one that would be good to check sizing with a muslin and adjust the warp width and length accordingly.

Finished dimensions: 27" (68.5 cm cm) long from top of shoulder to bottom of peplum, and 17" across (43 cm) from front center side to front center side.

Equipment: loom with 15" (38 cm) weaving width; for a shaft loom, sley 2 ends in an 8-dent reed. Use two 8-dent rigid-heddle reeds and 2 pick-up sticks if weaving on a rigid-heddle loom; shuttle, tapestry needle, sewing machine.

Warp yarn: *Silk City Fibers Bambu 7* (100% bamboo at 2,100 yd/lb [1,920 m/453 g], available on 1 lb [453 g] cones [1,920 m/453 g]) in Pearl White, 1,200 yd (1,097 m) or 1 cone needed.

Weft yarn: Same Bambu 7 used for warp, 1,145 yd (1,046 m) needed. For embroidered accent, we used Lotus Yarns Bamboo Soft from *Trendsetter* (100% bamboo, 990 yd/lb [905 m/453 g], 109 yd/ 1.75 oz[100 m/50 g] per skein), in color #16, Ocean Print, 10 yd (9.5 m) or 1 skein needed.

Weave structure: spot lace, huck lace, mock waffle weave, with on-loom embroidered weft accent.

Warp length: 5 yd (4.5 m), which includes take-up and 24" (61 cm) loom waste. If weaving on a shaft loom, allow 36" (91.5 cm) for loom waste and increase warp yarn yardage by a third.

Warp width: 15" (38 cm).

Number of warp ends: 240.

EPI: 16.

PPI: 16–17.

PICK-UP PATTERNS FOR BODICE, SIDE PANELS, AND PEPLUM:

Pattern 1: *bodice front and back in lace weave*

Pick-up stick pattern:
*1 up, 1 down; repeat from *.

Step 1: Down.

Step 2: Up and pick-up stick.

Step 3: Down.

Step 4: Up.

Repeat Steps 1–4 for pattern.

Pattern 2: *side panels in mock waffle weave*

Pick-up stick pattern:
*1 up, 2 down; repeat from *.

Step 1: Up.

Step 2: Pick-up stick.

Step 3: Up.

Step 4: Down.

Step 5: Up and pick-up stick.

Step 6: Down.

Step 7: Up and pick-up stick.

Step 8: Down.

Repeat Steps 1–8 for pattern.

Pattern 3: *peplum in spot lace*

Pick-up stick pattern A:
*4 up, 2 down; repeat from *.

Pick-up stick pattern B:
Pick up the first warp thread, then *2 down, 4 up; repeat from *.

Step 1: Up.

Step 2: Pick-up stick A.

Step 3: Up.

Step 4: Pick-up stick A.

Step 5: Up.

Step 6: Down.

Step 7: Up.

Step 8: Pick-up stick B.

Step 9: Up.

Step 10: Pick-up stick B.

Step 11: Up.

Step 12: Down.

Repeat these 12 steps for pattern.

WEAVING

Weave pattern 1 (lace) for a total of 42" (106.5 cm). For front, begin zigzag embroidery pattern after 1" (2.5 cm) of weaving and repeat 20 times (see page 133 for technique). Weave pattern 2 (mock waffle weave) for a total of 26" (66 cm). Weave pattern 3 (spot lace) for a total of 82" (208 cm). You'll have a tendency to overbeat, as you can pack this yarn in quite tightly. Your fabric will look a bit open on the loom but will full in the finishing process. Measure frequently to check that you're maintaining 15 to 16 ppi throughout.

FABRIC FINISHING

Secure edges of weaving with overhand knots. Handwash in warm, soapy water and lay flat to dry. Steam-press on low with a good deal of pressure.

ASSEMBLY

After washing, zigzag stitch between the panels before cutting apart. Zigzag at the end of one panel and the beginning of the next to prevent raveling on either side. Do not cut the front and back apart; they are a single piece (see cutting diagram on page 133).

Neck-hole: Create the V-neck

Step 1: Make a 9" × 6" (23 × 15 cm) triangle template to mark neck-hole (see diagram on page 133).

Step 2: Pin the template to the fabric, pinning so the 9" (23 cm) side of the triangle is at the shoulder ½" (1.3 cm) above the last embroidered accent. Find the vertical center of the front panel and match it with the center of the top of the triangle template.

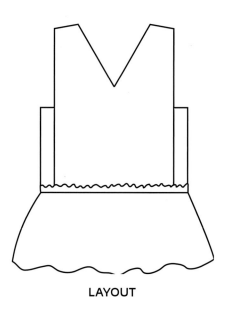

LAYOUT

PEPLUM DRAFT

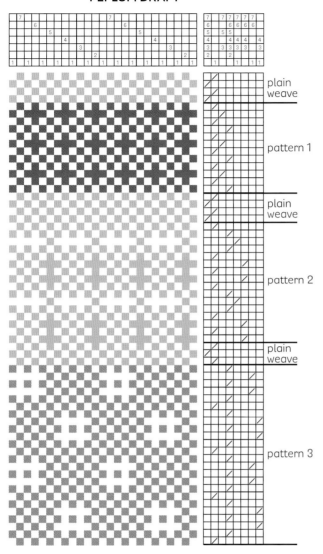

plain weave

pattern 1

plain weave

pattern 2

plain weave

pattern 3

Step 3: Straight stitch on the sewing machine along the edge of the template. Because the bamboo is slippery, straight stitch is better than zigzag in this case.

Step 4: Stitch a second triangle 1" (2.5 cm) on the inside of the one you just made.

Step 5: Stitch with a straight stitch on either side of the corners before snipping (see diagram on page 133).

Step 6: Cut out center triangle so that both stitch lines remain intact.

Step 7: Snip between securing lines to corners, stopping ⅛" (3 mm) from triangle points.

Step 8: Create ½" (1.3 cm) double rolled hems on all sides of the neck-hole opening. Press and pin.

Step 9: Topstitch on the right side along outer edge of neck-hole. Then, on the wrong side, stitch along the edge of the rolled hem.

Step 10: If the shoulder corners of your V-neck opening need stabilizing, whipstitch around the corners using a length of the Bambu yarn.

Side panels

Step 1: Cut the panels 9" (23 cm) wide, securing edge with zigzag stitch before cutting.

Step 2: Create ¼" (6 mm) rolled hems on any cut edges. Press, pin, and stitch.

Step 3: Repeat for panel 2.

Insert side panels

Step 1: On the front side, attach the side panel 7" (18 cm) down from the shoulder. On the back side, attach the side panel 8" (20.5 cm) down from shoulder. (7¾" [19.5 cm] of cloth should be exposed across the side at underarm tapering out to 8" [20.5 cm] at the bottom.)

Step 2: Hand baste and stitch leaving the bottom 2" (5 cm) unsewn on either side of the bottom of the side panels.

Step 3: Hem bottom edge of side panels with ¼" (6 mm) rolled hem so that the sides, front, and back edges are even across the bottom. If there is extra length left at the side panel, zigzag stitch and trim off the excess.

Step 4: Finish sewing the side seams where you left off.

Add the peplum

Step 1: Gather the peplum by pulling the second and third warp ends along one selvedge edge of the peplum. To prevent pulling the warp threads all the way through the fabric, at the other end, tie these 2 threads together in a bow.

Step 2: Check circumference of peplum to bodice and adjust the length accordingly.

Step 3: Pin and hand baste peplum to the right side of bottom edge of the bodice using a ½" (1.3 cm) overlap.

Step 4: Stitch the peplum to the bodice, starting and stopping 2" (5 cm) from either end to allow any adjusting of the fabric after it has been stitched to the bodice.

Step 5: After sewing, cut off any excess length at the ends of the fabric, secure with zigzag stitch before cutting, and create a ¼" (6 mm) single rolled hem edge on the right side of the fabric. Stitch remaining portion of hemmed edge to peplum top. For the other end, sew a ¼" (6 mm) hem on the wrong side. Top stitch the ends together.

Step 6: Stitch the remaining 2" (5 cm) sections left unsewn.

Step 7: Stitch the ends of the peplum together.

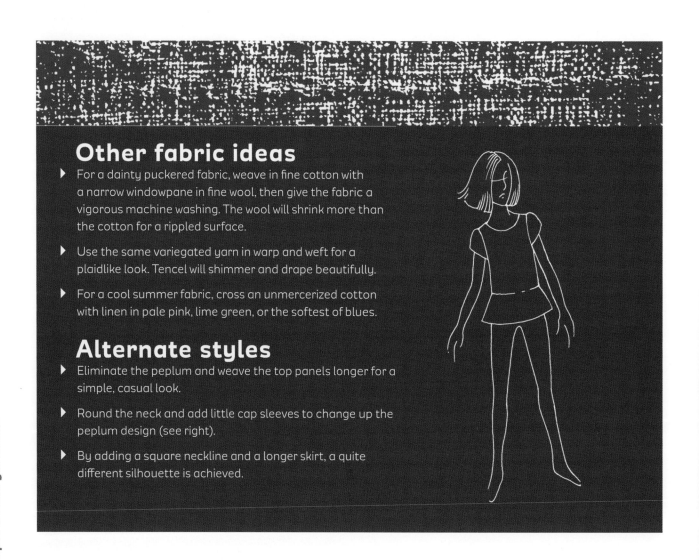

Other fabric ideas

▶ For a dainty puckered fabric, weave in fine cotton with a narrow windowpane in fine wool, then give the fabric a vigorous machine washing. The wool will shrink more than the cotton for a rippled surface.

▶ Use the same variegated yarn in warp and weft for a plaidlike look. Tencel will shimmer and drape beautifully.

▶ For a cool summer fabric, cross an unmercerized cotton with linen in pale pink, lime green, or the softest of blues.

Alternate styles

▶ Eliminate the peplum and weave the top panels longer for a simple, casual look.

▶ Round the neck and add little cap sleeves to change up the peplum design (see right).

▶ By adding a square neckline and a longer skirt, a quite different silhouette is achieved.

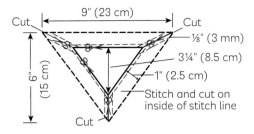

NECK-HOLE TEMPLATE

9" (23 cm)

Cut — Cut

⅛" (3 mm)

3¼" (8.5 cm)

6" (15 cm)

1" (2.5 cm)

Stitch and cut on
inside of stitch line

Cut

- - - - - - = straight stitch

✂ = cut

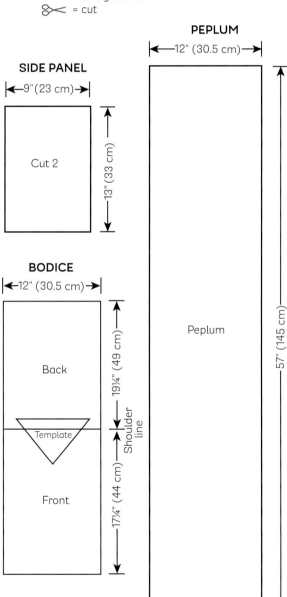

PEPLUM

12" (30.5 cm)

SIDE PANEL

9" (23 cm)

Cut 2

13" (33 cm)

Peplum

57" (145 cm)

BODICE

12" (30.5 cm)

Back

Template

Front

36½" (92.5 cm)

19¼" (49 cm)

Shoulder line

17¼" (44 cm)

EMBROIDERY ON THE LOOM

The woven web under tension is the perfect base for embroidery, especially when worked on a textured weave such as allover lace. With needle and thread, you can use the floats as guides for weaving in and out of them to stitch a pattern. An embroidered technique will appear more on the surface, and when combined with the weave structure, a pattern-on-pattern effect can be achieved. For more pattern ideas, see *The Weaver's Idea Book*, pages 200–201.

Step 1: Begin by leaving a tail that will be sewn in on the back side after the weaving is removed from the loom. Or, if the end will be encased in a rolled hem, the end can be left hanging and trimmed after washing.

Step 2: Sew in and out of the floats to create a pattern. In this case, we've started at the edge and stepped over one long float and up one row, repeating this and then reversing for a zigzag pattern (**Figure 1**).

Because the embroidery yarn would be quite long if carried up the selvedge when we moved from row to row, we cut it after each row, always working right to left. Alternately, you can carry the yarn under the weaving. When a yarn runs out, we like to end and begin at the selvedge (**Figure 2**).

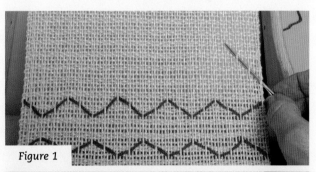

Figure 1

Figure 2

Casual, yet fancy enough for a cocktail party, our Swing Top sports cap sleeves, an accent placket on the front, and an uneven hemline that dips down in the back. A box pleat in the back gives this top its swing. Two warps are required: one for the body and the other for the cap sleeves. Alternately, you could plan a longer warp and weave the cap sleeves on the same warp, though you'll be missing out on the contrast the two warps provide.

SWING TOP

Designed and woven by *Sara Goldenberg*

Two beautifully dyed colors of yarn, woven in a petite check and complementary stripes, are the makings for this enchanting fabric. We threaded up two different stripe patterns in the warp for a smaller check at the sides and a wider one in the center. For the back, we wove with a single color for stripes. This is one of the advantages of handweaving your own cloth. You can weave several variations on the same warp and mix and match them in the construction.

Body

Garment size: medium.

Finished dimensions: 23" (58. 5 cm) across, 23" (58.5 cm) from top of shoulder to bottom on the front, and 28½" (72.5 cm) from top of shoulder to the bottom on the back.

Equipment: loom with 25" (63.5 cm) weaving width. For a rigid-heddle loom, use two 12-dent heddles; 2 shuttles, sewing machine.

Warp yarn: *SweetGeorgia Merino Silk Lace*, hand-dyed yarn (50% merino/50% silk at 3,477 yd/lb [3,179 m/453 g], 760 yd/3.5 oz [700 m/100 g] per skein) in Lettuce Wrap, 700 yd [640 m] or 1 skein needed; and Tourmaline, 685 yd [626 m] or 1 skein needed.

Weft yarn: *SweetGeorgia Cashsilk Lace*, hand-dyed yarn (55% silk/45% cashmere at 3,657 yd/lb [3,344 m/453 g], 400 yd/1.75 oz [365 m/50 g] per skein) in Lettuce Wrap, 200 yd (183 m) or 1 skein needed; and Tourmaline, 520 yd (475.5 m) or 2 skeins needed.

Weave structure: plain weave.

Warp length: 2⅕ yd (2 m), which includes take-up and 24" (61 cm) loom waste. If weaving on a shaft loom, allow 36" (91.5 cm) for loom waste and increase warp yarn yardage by a third.

Warp width: 24¾" (63 cm).

Number of warp ends: 594.

EPI: 24.

PPI: 15–16.

Warp color order:

	12x	13x		11x	End	
Lettuce Wrap	6		12	6	6	300
Tourmaline		6		12	6	294
				Total warp ends		594

WEAVING

Weave a check. Weave 7–8 picks or ½" (1.3 cm) of Lettuce Wrap. Weave 7–8 picks or ½" (1.3 cm) of Tourmaline. Repeat for 32" (81.5 cm). Weave the remainder of the warp, 26" (66 cm), using Tourmaline.

FABRIC FINISHING

Secure ends with overhand knots and lightly full by hand in warm, soapy water. Rinse in cool water and lay flat to dry. Steam-press.

Cap sleeves and placket

Finished dimensions:
4" (10 cm) wide and 13¾" (35 cm) where the sleeve attaches to the garment.

Equipment: 12-dent reed, 1 shuttle.

Warp and weft yarns:
SweetGeorgia Cashsilk Lace, hand-dyed yarn (55% silk/45% cashmere at 3,657 yd/lb [3,344 m/453 g], 400 yd/1.75 oz [366 m/50 g] per skein) in Lettuce Wrap, 192 yd (176 m) needed for warp (warp yarns are used doubled), and 60 yd (55 m) needed for weft (yarn is used singly in the weft).

Total yardage for warp and weft: 252 yd (231 m) or 1 skein needed.

Weave structure: plain weave.

Warp length: 2 yd (1.8 m), which includes take-up and 24" (61 cm) loom waste. If weaving on a shaft loom, allow 36" (91.5 cm) for loom waste and increase warp yarn yardage by a third.

Warp width: 4" (10 cm).

Number of warp ends: 48 working ends (96 actual ends) doubled in the warp.

EPI: 12.

PPI: 10.

WEAVING

Weave in plain weave using a single strand of Cashsilk until the warp runs out, about 44" (112 cm).

FABRIC FINISHING

Secure ends with overhand knots, handwash in warm water and mild soap. Lay flat to dry and steam-press.

ASSEMBLY

Body

Step 1: Zigzag stitch on both ends of the fabric and cut off fringe.

Step 2: Zigzag stitch at end of front and back panels (stripes and checks) and cut apart.

Step 3: Create a ¼" (6 mm) double rolled hem on one end of front (checked) panel.

Step 4: Make a single ¼" (6 mm) fold on the other end on the wrong side of the fabric and stitch into place. This will lap at the back and does not need a double rolled hem (eliminates bulk).

Step 5: Create neck hole (see template below). Line up the template so that the back of neck hole is 3½" (1.3 cm) down from the back edge of cloth (end with a single ¼" [6 mm] hem) and centered from side to side, page 138.

Step 6: Zigzag stitch around the neck-hole template and then again ¾" (2 cm) in from the initial stitch line. Straight stitch on either side of snip lines (see diagram below). Cut out interior circle. Fold edges under to make a double rolled hem. Press, pin, and stitch.

Step 7: Make a single ¼" (6 mm) hem at the top of the back panel on the right side of the fabric. This will be hidden by the front piece lapping over the top of it. Steam-press and machine straight stitch.

Step 8: Make the box pleat. Find the center of the back (striped fabric) on the end with ¼" (6 mm) fold. On the right side, mark with a pin measuring out 1½" (3.8 cm)

on either side of the centerline.

Step 9: Fold the outside points into the center and pin. Hand baste first, then straight stitch.

Step 10: Make the armholes (see template below). Lay the garment flat, right side up. Place the armhole template on top of the fabric with the curved edge facing the neck-hole. Line the center of the template up with the outermost edge of neck hole, 5" (13 cm) from edge of top plaid fabric (portion seen on back of the top) and 4" (10 cm) away from neck hole.

Step 11: Zigzag stitch around the edge of the template. Remove the template and stitch another securing line using a straight stitch ½" (1.3 cm) in from zigzag and moving toward the selvedge edge of the cloth.

Step 12: Create a ¼" (6 mm) rolled hem. For this edge, create 3 folds, like a double rolled hem. This extra fold will add strength to the armhole for the cap sleeve attachment. Steam-press, pin, and stitch.

Step 13: Sew side seams with a ½" (1.3 cm) seam allowance. With right sides together, line up lower

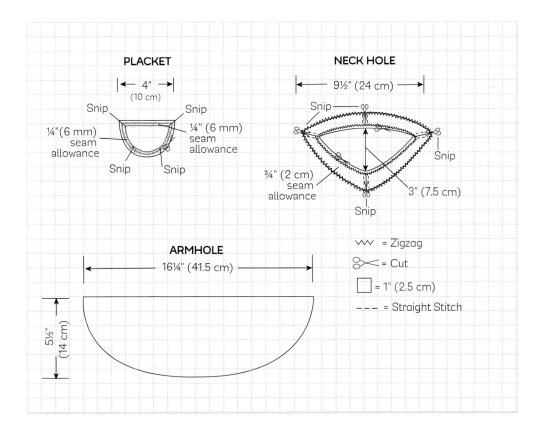

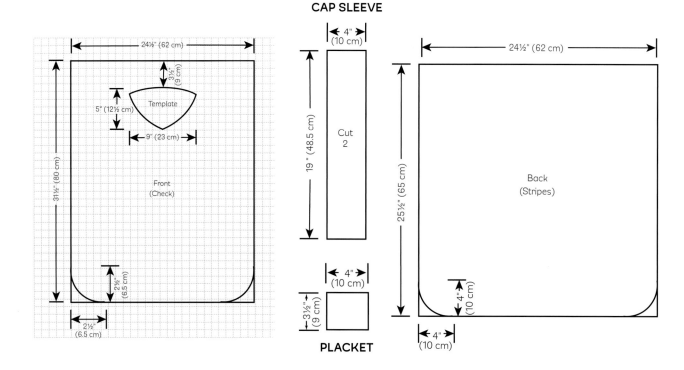

corners of armhole opening. This will be where you begin stitching. Stop side seam 2½" (6.5 cm) before end of front panel. The back will hang down lower than the front.

Step 14: Round the corners of the front and back. On the front corners, start rounding at the seam allowance and end 2½" (6.5 cm) in from the edge of the garment. On the back of the garment, start at seam allowance and end 4" (10 cm) in from the edge of the cloth. You may find it helpful to make a template for the corners.

Step 15: Pin front corner template to one side of the front panel. Zigzag stitch around template. Straight stitch ¾" (2 cm) outside the zigzag line. Straight stitch on either side of snip lines. There will be a triangle of excess fabric from where the curve was created. Cut away excess cloth, leaving all stitch lines intact. Repeat on other side of the front. Repeat these steps with the larger template on back panel.

Step 16: Snip at snip lines on all 4 rounded corners and create double rolled hems. Steam-press, pin, and stitch around the curve starting from where the rolled hem intersects the curve. Stitch hem in place ¼" (6 mm)

from the edge of the curve. Stitch slowly and turn fabric to keep an even distance from the edge of the cloth.

Step 17: Create the cap sleeves and placket. Secure with zigzag stitch and cut off 4½" (11.5 cm) of cloth for the placket. Again, secure the edges with zigzag stitch and cut 2, pieces for the cap sleeves each 19" (48.5 cm) long.

Step 18: Using 2 warp yarns ½" (1.3 cm) in from edge, pull cap sleeve cloth into a ruffle. Pull from both sides. Once desired ruffle amount is obtained, tie a double knot on either end of the pulled warp threads. Leave ¾" (2 cm) of fabric on either side without ruffle. Secure with a zigzag stitch. Measure second sleeve to match first sleeve in length before attaching.

Step 19: Once caps are created, find the center of the cap and the top of the shoulder in the shirt. Pin the ruffled edge of the cap sleeve to the wrong side of the sleeve opening. Pulling the warp turns a straight piece of cloth into a curved piece.

Step 20: Angle the bottom edges of the cap sleeves so that they stop 3¼" (8.25 cm) above the bottom of the armhole. Handstitch the sleeves into place. Do not stitch down ¾" (2 cm) edges of sleeves. Once the cap sleeve is attached, steam-press ¾" (2 cm) area under, creating a single fold. Handstitch into place on both edges of each sleeve.

Placket

Step 1: Using cap sleeve/placket fabric (see template, page 137), stitch around template with a zigzag stitch.

Step 2: Stitch another row of zigzag ¼" (6 mm) outside the first stitch line.

Step 3: Stitch on either side of the snip lines with straight stitch.

Step 4: Cut out, leaving all of the stitching intact.

Step 5: Make snips and steam-press the edges under ¼" (6 mm) all the way around the placket.

Step 6: Stitch the top of placket to the shirt 6½" (16.5 cm) down from the shoulder and 3¾" (9.5 cm)

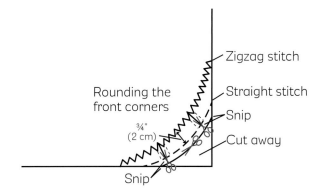

Rounding the front corners

¾" (2 cm)

Zigzag stitch

Straight stitch

Snip

Cut away

Snip

in from armhole on the left side of shirt. Line up the top straight edge of the placket with the beginning or end of a checked block. Handstitch or use a machine and stitch the top edge. Handstitch the curved portion of the placket to the shirt being careful to keep the grain of the cloth in line with the grain of the shirt.

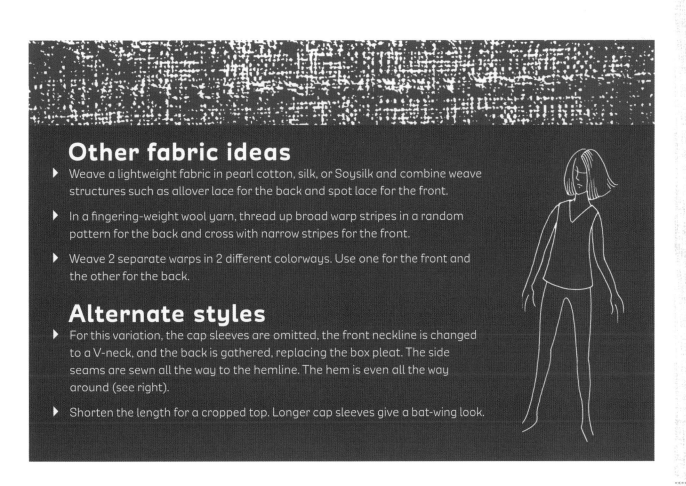

Other fabric ideas

▶ Weave a lightweight fabric in pearl cotton, silk, or Soysilk and combine weave structures such as allover lace for the back and spot lace for the front.

▶ In a fingering-weight wool yarn, thread up broad warp stripes in a random pattern for the back and cross with narrow stripes for the front.

▶ Weave 2 separate warps in 2 different colorways. Use one for the front and the other for the back.

Alternate styles

▶ For this variation, the cap sleeves are omitted, the front neckline is changed to a V-neck, and the back is gathered, replacing the box pleat. The side seams are sewn all the way to the hemline. The hem is even all the way around (see right).

▶ Shorten the length for a cropped top. Longer cap sleeves give a bat-wing look.

GLOSSARY OF WEAVING AND SEWING TERMS

Accordion pleat. A fold made by doubling a fabric back onto itself at regular intervals.

Apron bars. The bars that are connected to both the cloth beam and warp beam with apron cords to which the warp is tied.

Backstitch. Sewing in reverse at the beginning and end of a line of machine stitching to secure the end of the stitching. Also, a handstitching technique.

Balanced weave. Fabric in which the number of warp ends per inch is the same as the number of weft ends per inch.

Beat. To push the weft threads into place with the reed.

Box pleats. Back-to-back pleats that swing outward.

Brooks bouquet. A hand-manipulated weaving technique worked on an open shed in which groups of raised threads are encircled with weft. Plain weave is woven between rows of bouquets.

Butt join. Two edges joined but not overlapping that are whipstitched together.

Cross. The figure-eight made at one end of the warp when measuring. It keeps the warp ends in order and helps prevent tangles.

Direct-peg warping. A method of warping the rigid-heddle loom in which the warp is measured around a single peg and threaded through the reed in the same step.

Double rolled hem. An edge finished by turning the fabric under once and then again. It may be stitched by hand or machine.

End. One warp yarn (or thread).

EPI (ends per inch). The number of warp threads in 1 inch.

Fell line. The place on the loom where unwoven warp and web (or woven cloth) meet.

Felting. The irreversible process of binding fibers together (usually wool).

Fiber. The substance, such as wool, from which yarn is spun.

Finishing. The final process in making a woven fabric. After the fabric is removed from the loom, it needs to be washed, dried in the dryer, or ironed, or a combination of the three.

Ghiordes knot. A knot used to make pile. Also, a rya knot.

Hemstitching. A stitching technique used to protect the weft at the beginning and end of a weaving. It can also be used decoratively within a fabric.

Loom. A frame that holds the warp taut for weaving.

Loom waste. Any yarn that is not woven at the beginning and end of a warp.

Novelty yarn. Generally a fancy, complex yarn that has different twists, irregularities, and fibers.

Pick. One row of weaving. Also called a shot.

Pick and pick. When 2 colors alternate in the weft (i.e., 1 row of white, 1 row of red, 1 row of white, 1 row of red, and so on).

Pick-up. The technique of holding warp threads out of the way to create floats in weaving.

Pick-up stick. A narrow stick used to pick up patterns. It can be turned on edge to form a shed. Also called a shed stick.

Plain weave. The simplest of all weaves; an over, under, over, under interlacement.

Plied yarn. Yarn that is composed of several single strands of yarn twisted together.

PPI (picks per inch). The number of weft rows, or picks, in 1 inch of weaving.

Reed. On a shaft loom, the metal comblike frame in the beater that determines sett and beats the weft into place. Also used to refer to the rigid-heddle reed on a rigid-heddle loom. On a rigid-heddle loom, the reed determines sett, beats the weft into place, and is raised or lowered to create the shed for the shuttle to pass through.

Rising shed loom. A loom in which shafts are lifted to create the shed.

Rolled hem or double rolled hem. Folding the edge of the fabric under 2 times to form a hem that hides any raw edges.

Selvedge. The edge threads in weaving.

Sett. Number of warp ends in 1 inch.

Shed. The space between raised and lowered warp threads through which the shuttle passes during weaving.

Shed stick. Narrow stick used to make a shed; also called a pick-up stick.

Shuttle. The tool that holds weft yarn for weaving and carries the weft back and forth through the shed during weaving.

Singles yarn. A yarn made of one strand; not a plied yarn.

Sley. To thread the warp threads through the reed, generally with a threading hook.

Soumak. A finger-controlled technique worked on a closed shed in which the weft encircles groups of warp threads. Plain weave is woven in between rows of soumak.

Tabby. A plain-weave ground that binds pattern picks.

Threading hook. A long, flat metal hook with a handle used to thread the reed.

Warp. The set of threads held taut by a loom.

Warp-dominant. Refers to fabric in which the warp shows more than the weft.

Warping. The process of putting the warp on the loom.

Warping board. A rectangular frame fitted with dowels that is used to measure the warp.

Warping peg. A single peg that is clamped to a table and used to measure warp in the direct-warping method.

Weaver's angle. The angle at which the weft is inserted into the shed to allow for take-up caused by the weft yarn traveling over and under warp threads, rather than in a straight line. Generally, a 30-degree angle is used.

Weaving. Crossing one set of threads with another. The warps are those threads that are held taut by a loom. The weft threads cross the warp.

Web. On the loom, the warp that has been already woven; woven fabric.

Weft. The threads that cross the warp.

Weft-dominant. Refers to fabric in which the weft is prominent but does not completely cover the warp.

Weft-faced. Refers to fabric in which only the weft shows.

Weft protector. Any of the finishing processes that prevent the weft from raveling. Examples are hemstitching, tied fringe, twisted fringe, and overhand knots.

Yarn. Continuous fibers that have been spun or constructed.

YARN CHART

MAKING SUBSTITUTIONS

To help you make substitutions, we've included a yarn chart of all the yarns we've used in the projects. The most successful way to substitute a yarn is to find one similar in style, size, and fiber content. Choosing a yarn as close as possible to what we used for a project will ensure that your result will be as close as possible to our design.

These yarns are shown life size. To check the size of your yarn, lay your yarn on top of the one you're trying to match to see how close it is in size.

Check the content as well, because yarns with different fiber contents will behave differently. Try for a similar fiber or fiber blend.

Additionally, consider the style of the project yarn and look for a yarn with a similar structure.

The final element to making a substitution is to compare the yardage of one yarn to the next. We've provided the yards per pound for all yarns, as this is an easy way to compare yarn to yarn (because put-ups vary so widely).

V Shawl, page 22
Classic Elite Chalet, 70% baby alpaca/30% bamboo viscose, 891 yd/lb (815 m/453 g). Color: 7416 Parchment

Classic Elite Chalet, 70% baby alpaca/30% bamboo viscose, 891 yd/lb (815 m/453 g). Color: 7477 Charcoal.

Ruffled Shawl, page 28
SweetGeorgia Merino Silk Aran, 50% merino wool/50% silk, 840 yd/lb [768 m/453 g]. Color: Cayenne.

SweetGeorgia Merino Silk Aran, 50% merino wool/50% silk, 840 yd/lb [768 m/453 g]. Color: Cypress.

SweetGeorgia Merino Silk Fine, 50% merino/50% silk, 1,727 yd/lb [1,579m/453 g]. Color: Autumn Flame.

SweetGeorgia Merino Silk Fine, 50% merino/50% silk, 1,727 yd/lb [1,579m/453 g]. Color: Cayenne.

SweetGeorgia Merino Silk Lace, 50% merino/50% silk, 3,477 yd/lb [3,179m/453 g]. Color: Autumn Flame.

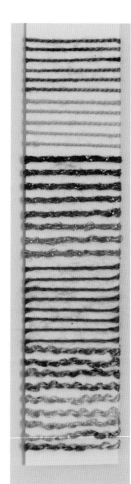

Starry, Starry Night, page 34
Interlacements Soya, 100% Soysilk, 2-ply, 3,600 yd/lb [3,291 m/453 g]. Color: Forest Floor.

Interlacements Soya, 100% Soysilk, 2-ply, 3,600 yd/lb [3,291 m/453 g]. Color: Blue Green.

Interlacements Irish Jig, 40% flax/31% cotton/29% rayon with metallic thread, novelty yarn, 1,200 yd/lb [1,097 m/453 g]. Color: Oceans.

Skacel Fil Royal, 100% baby alpaca, 3,017 yd/lb [2,758 m/453 g], singles yarn. Color: #3515, Blue Spruce.

Interlacements Zig Zag, 98% rayon/2% nylon, 1,450 yd/lb [1,326 m/453,g], crepe yarn. Color: Submarine.

Green-Gray Topper, page 40

Alpaca with a Twist Fino, 70% baby alpaca/30% silk, 3,972 yd/lb [3,632 m/453 g]. Color: #0098, Silver Belle.

Trendsetter Kid Seta, 70% mohair/30% silk, 405 yd/lb [370 m/453 g]. Color: #368, Olive.

Cowl-Neck Sweater, page 52

Berroco Voyage, 93% alpaca/7% polyester, 1,143 yd/lb [1,045 m/453 g]. Color: #4015, Coastline.

Berroco Seduce, 47% rayon/25% viscose/17% linen/11% silk, 1,135 yd/lb [1,038 m/453 g]. Color: #4437.

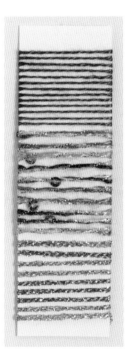

Honeycomb Boatneck Top, page 46

WEBS 8/2 Tencel, 3,360 yd/lb [3,072 m/453 g]. Color: Shale.

Tahki-Stacy Charles Inc. Adele, 43% viscose/28% polyester/20% kid mohair/9% polyamide, 1,545 yd/lb [1,415 m/453 g]. Color: #24, Gold.

Crystal Olympus from EmmaCreations, 100% polyester, 3,163 yd/lb [2,892 m/453 g]. Color: #7.

Tabard, page 56

Brown Sheep Nature Spun, sportweight, 100% wool, 2,355 yd/lb [2,154 m/453 g]. Color: #N46 Red Fox.

Brown Sheep Nature Spun, sport-weight, 100% wool, 2,355 yd/lb [2,154 m/453 g]. Color: #145 Salmon.

Brown Sheep Wildfoote, sock yarn, 75% washable wool/25% nylon, 1,966 yd/lb [1,825 m/kg]. Color: #SY150, Acappella.

Brown Sheep Wildfoote, sock yarn, 75% washable wool/25% nylon, 1,966 yd/lb [1,825 m/kg]. Color: #SY600, Symphony.

Camisole, page 62

Shibui Staccato, 65% superwash merino/30% silk/5% nylon, 1,746 yd/lb [1,597 m/453 g]. Color: #111, Bordeaux.

Shibui Sock, 100% superwash merino, 1,746 yd/lb [1,597 m/453 g]. Color: #1395, Honey.

Mountain Meadows Wool Lilura, 3-ply fingering-weight, 50% merino/50% alpaca-merino blend, 2,133 yd/lb [1,950 m/453 g]. Color: Sorrel.

Cape with Collar, page 74

Nirvana from Filatura Di Crosa, Tahki-Stacy Charles Inc., 100% superwash merino wool, 6,764 yd/lb [6,185 m/453 g]. Color: 35, gray.

Gioiello Fancy from Filatura Di Crosa, Tahki-Stacy Charles Inc., 30% kid mohair/30% wool/20% polyamide/10% cotton/10% polyester, 1,829 yd/lb [1,672 m/453 g]. Color: 69.

Superior from Filatura Di Crosa, Tahki-Stacy Charles Inc., 70% cashmere/25% silk/5% merino wool, 5,964 yd/lb [5,453 m/453 g]. Color: 73.

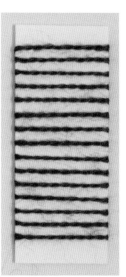

Classic Capelet, page 68

Isager 2 fingering-weight, 50% alpaca/50% wool, 2,483 yd/lb [2,270 m/453 g]. Color: #47, Blue Gray.

Fall Blaze Shrug, page 78

Mountain Colors Half Crepe, 100% merino wool, 1,680 yd/lb [1,536 m/453 g]. Color: Hummingbird.

Mountain Colors Half Crepe, 100% merino wool, 1,680 yd/lb [1,536 m/453 g]. Color: Marigold.

Mountain Colors Merino Ribbon, 80% superfine merino wool/20% nylon, 980 yd/lb [896 m/453 g]. Color: Spring Eclipse.

Mountain Colors 4/8's Wool, 100% wool, 1,145 yd/lb [1,047 m/453 g]. Color: Hummingbird.

Good Earth Ruana, page 84

Plymouth Yarn Encore Chunky, 75% acrylic/25% wool, 654 yd/lb [598 m/453 g]. Color: #1405, gray-green.

Tahki Yarns Juno, 97% alpaca/3% nylon, 770 yd/lb [704 m/453 g]. Color: #07, Paprika.

Classic Elite Yarns Liberty Wool, 100% washable wool, 1,115 yd/lb [1,019 m/453 g]. Color: #7899, Cloudy Dawn.

Trendsetter Checkmate, 80% polyamide/20% nylon ribbon, 640 yd/lb [585 m/453 g]. Color: #603, Harvest.

Lorna's Laces Pearl, 51% silk/49% bamboo, 636 yd/lb [582 m/453 g]. Color: 50NS, Poppy.

Ironstone Big Loop Mohair, 90% mohair/5% wool/5% nylon, 600 yd/lb [549 m/453 g]. Color: Shade, #251(E).

Brown Sheep Lamb's Pride, Worsted, 85% wool/15% mohair, 760 yd/lb [695 m/453 g]. Color: #M-07, Sable.

Flame Lace Top, page 90

Interlacements 2-ply Hemp, 100% hemp at 4,190 yd/lb [3,831 m/453 g]. Color: Colorado Treasures.

WEBSValley Fibers 8/2 Tencel, 100% Tencel at 3,360 yd/lb [3,072 m/453 g]. Color: Fire.

WEBSValley Fibers 8/2 Tencel, 100% Tencel at 3,360 yd/lb [3,072 m/453 g]. Color: Pompeii.

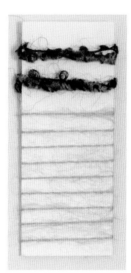

Turtleneck Tunic, page 96

Interlacements Yarns Velvet, 70% rayon/30% mohair, 700 yd/lb [640 m/453 g]. Color: Navy Blue.

Shibui Knits Yarn Silk Cloud, 60% kid mohair/40% silk, 6,000 yd/lb [5,486 m/453 g]. Color: #2024 Lime.

Sweater Jacket, page 102

Interlacements Rick Rack, 100% rayon, 1,200 yd/lb [1,097 m/453 g]. Color: Desert Lichen.

Skacel Kid Paillettes, 42% kid mohair /40% polyester/18% silk, 2,490 yd/lb [2,277 m/453 g]. Color: #380, Mauve.

Interlacements Cabled Cotton, 100% mercerized cotton, 1,125 yd/lb [1,029 m/453 g]. Color: Fireplace Embers.

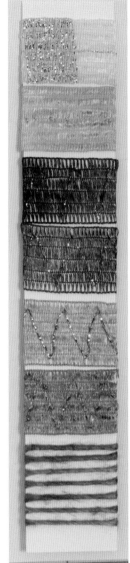

Ribbon T-Top, page 108

Prism Yarn Galaxy, hand-dyed ribbon, 95% nylon/5% metallic polyester, 432 yd/lb [395 m/453 g]. Color: Sierra.

Prism Yarn Constellation, hand-dyed ribbon, 95% nylon/5% metallic polyester, 432 yd/lb [395 m/453 g]. Color: Twilight.

Prism Yarn Constellation Layers, hand-dyed ribbon, 95% nylon/5% metallic polyester, 432 yd/lb [395 m/453 g]. Color: Bracken.

Prism Yarn Petite Madison Layers, hand-dyed yarn, 75% merino wool/15% cashmere/10% silk at 1,690 yd/lb [1,545 m/453 g]. Color: Platinum.

Hoodie, page 114

Berroco Blackstone Tweed, 65% wool/25% mohair/10% angora, 1,188 yd/lb [1,086 m/453 g]. Color: #2603, Ancient Mariner.

Berroco Blackstone Tweed, 65% wool/25% mohair/10% angora, 1,188 yd/lb [1,086 m/453 g]. Color: #2663, Marsh.

Berroco Ultra Alpaca, 50% alpaca/50% wool at 983 yd/lb [900 m/453 g]. Color: #6211, Duncan.

Berroco Ultra Alpaca Light, 50% alpaca/50% wool, 1,316 yd/lb [1,203 m/453 g]. Color: #4294, Turquoise Mix.

Berroco Ultra Alpaca Light, 50% alpaca/50% wool, 1,316 yd/lb [1,203 m/453 g]. Color: #4275, Pea Soup Mix.

Ode to Coco, page 120

Trendsetter Twiggy, 47% linen/32% viscose/21% polyamide, 773 yd/lb [707 m/453 g]. Color: #103, Cream Puff.

Trendsetter Twiggy, 47% linen/32% viscose/21% polyamide, 773 yd/lb [707 m/453 g]. Color: #92, Mushroom Soup.

Trendsetter Zoe, 50% cotton/45% viscose/5% polyester, 682 yd/lb [624 m/453 g]. Color: Apple Pie.

Trendsetter Summit, 44% wool/44% acrylic/12% nylon, 1,006/yd/lb [920 m/453 g]. Color: #4202.

Trendsetter Dune, 45% mohair/25% acrylic/20% viscose/6% wool/4% polyester, 791 yd/lb [723 m/453 g]. Color: #124.

Trendsetter Luna, 100% polyester, 6,588 yd/lb [6,024 m/453 g]. Color: #100, Gold.

Trendsetter Merino and Shadow, 100% merino, 915 yd/lb [837 m/453 g]. Color: #126.

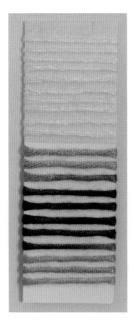

Peplum, page 128

Silk City Fibers Bambu 7, 100% bamboo, 2,100 yd/lb [1,920 m/453 g]. Color: Pearl White.

Lotus Yarns Bamboo Soft from Trendsetter, 100% bamboo, 990 yd/lb [905 m/453 g]. Color: #16, Ocean Print.

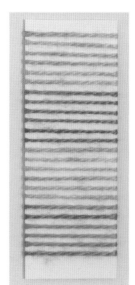

Swing Top, page 134

SweetGeorgia Merino Silk Lace, hand-dyed yarn, 50% merino/50% silk, 3,477 yd/lb [3,179 m/453 g]. Color: Lettuce Wrap.

SweetGeorgia Merino Silk Lace, hand-dyed yarn, 50% merino/50% silk, 3,477 yd/lb [3,179 m/453 g]. Color: Tourmaline.

SweetGeorgia Cashsilk Lace, hand-dyed yarn, 55% silk/45% cashmere, 3,657 yd/lb [3,344 m/453 g]. Color: Lettuce Wrap.

SweetGeorgia Cashsilk Lace, hand-dyed yarn, 55% silk/45% cashmere, 3,657 yd/lb [3,344 m/453 g]. Color: Tourmaline.

BIBLIOGRAPHY

Aimone, Katherine Duncan. *The Fiberarts Book of Wearable Art.* Asheville, North Carolina: Lark Books, 2002.

Alderman, Sharon D., and Kathryn Wertenberger. *Handwoven, Tailormade.* Loveland, Colorado: Interweave, 1982.

Baizerman, Suzanne, and Karen Searle. *Finishes in the Ethnic Tradition.* St. Paul, Minnesota: Dos Tejedoras, 1978.

Beard, Betty J. *Fashions from the Loom.* Loveland, Colorado: Interweave, 1980.

Colton, Virginia, editor. *Reader's Digest Complete Guide to Needlework*, 8th edition. Pleasantville, New York/Montreal: Readers Digest Association, 1984.

Davenport, Betty Linn. *Hands On Rigid Heddle Weaving.* Loveland, Colorado: Interweave, 1987.

———. *Textures and Patterns for the Rigid Heddle Loom*, revised edition. Battle Ground, Washington: Betty Linn Davenport, distributed by Fine Fiber Press, 2008.

Gipson, Liz. *Weaving Made Easy.* Loveland, Colorado: Interweave, 2008.

Hart, Rowena. *The Ashford Book of Rigid Heddle Weaving.* Ashburton, New Zealand: Ashford Handicrafts, 2002.

Howard, Sarah, and Elisabeth Kendrick. *Creative Weaving: Beautiful Fabrics with a Simple Loom.* Asheville, North Carolina: Lark Books, 2008.

Iwamura, Misao. *Plain Weaving: Try Creating Original Textiles Using Plain Weaving.* Tokyo: Bunko, 2002. English translation distributed in the United States by Habu Textiles.

Lamb, Sara. *Woven Treasures: One-of-a-Kind Bags With Folk Weaving Techniques.* Loveland, Colorado: Interweave, 2009.

Mayer, Anita Luvera. *Clothing From the Hands That Weave.* Loveland, Colorado: Interweave, 1984.

Menz, Deb. *Color Works.* Loveland, Colorado: Interweave, 2004.

Murphy, Marilyn. *Woven to Wear.* Loveland, Colorado: Interweave, 2013.

Patrick, Jane. *The Weaver's Idea Book.* Loveland, Colorado: Interweave, 2010.

———, ed. *Handwoven's Design Collection 6: Not for Beginners Only.* Loveland, Colorado: Interweave, 1983.

———, ed. *Handwoven's Design Collection 7: Simple Styles.* Loveland, Colorado: Interweave, 1985.

———, ed. *Handwoven's Design Collection 9: No-Sew Garments.* Loveland, Colorado: Interweave, 1986.

Patrick, Jane, and Stephanie Flynn Sokolov. *Woven Scarves.* Loveland, Colorado: Interweave, 2014.

Stockton, James. *Designer's Guide to Color.* San Francisco: Chronicle Books, 1984.

Stuvel, Pieke. *A Touch of Style.* Middlesex, England: Penguin Books, 1981.

Sutton, Ann. *Colour-and-Weave Design: A Practical Reference Book.* England: Sterling, 1985.

Sutton, Ann, and Diane Sheehan. *Ideas in Weaving.* Asheville, North Carolina: Lark Books, 1982.

Takekura, Masaaki, publisher. *Suke Suke.* Tokyo: Nuno Corporation, 1997.

Tidball, Harriet. *Surface Interest: Textiles of Today: Shuttle Craft Monograph Two.* Lansing, Michigan: The Shuttle Craft Guild, 1961.

———. *Undulating Weft Effects: Shuttle Craft Monograph Nine.* Freeland, Washington: HTH, 1963.

———. *Two-Harness Textiles: The Loom-Controlled Weaves: Shuttle Craft Monograph Twenty.* Santa Ana, California: HTH, 1967.

West, Virginia. *Finishing Touches for the Handweaver.* Loveland, Colorado: Interweave, 1988.

SOURCES FOR YARNS

Alpaca Fiber Cooperative of
North America, Inc.
17494 State Hwy. 58N
Decatur, TN 37322
afcna.com

Alpaca with a Twist
950 South White River
Pkwy. W. Dr.
Indianapolis, IN 46221
alpacawithatwist.com

Berroco
1 Tupperware Dr., Ste. 4
N. Smithfield, RI 02896
berroco.com

Brown Sheep Company
100662 County Rd. 16
Mitchell, NE 69357
brownsheep.com

Classic Elite Yarns
16 Esquire Rd., Unit 2
N. Billerica, MA 01962
classiceliteyarns.com

EmmaCreation
30011 Ivy Glenn Dr., Ste. 122
Laguna Niguel, CA 92677
emmacreation.com

Interlacements Yarns
3250 Froelich Rd.
Abrams, WI 54101
interlacementsyarns.com

Ironstone Yarns
5401 San Diego Rd. NE
Albuquerque, NM 87113
info@ironstoneonline.com

Isager
Tutto Santa Fe
10 Domingo Rd.
Santa Fe, NM 87508
knitisager.com

Koigu Wool Designs
Box 158
Chatsworth, ON
Canada N0H 1G0
koigu.com

Lorna's Laces
4229 North Honore St.
Chicago, IL 60613
lornaslaces.net

Louet North America
3425 Hands Rd.
Prescott, ON
Canada K0E 1T0
louet.com

Mountain Colors
PO Box 156
Corvallis, MT 59828
mountaincolors.com

Mountain Meadow Wool
22 Plains Dr.
Buffalo, WY 82834
mountainmeadowwool.com

Plymouth Yarn Company
500 Lafayette St.
Bristol, PA 19007
plymouthyarn.com

Prism Yarn
3140 39th Ave. N.
St. Petersburg, FL 33714
prismyarn.com

Shibui Knits, LLC
1500 NW 18th, Ste. 110
Portland, OR 97209
shibuiknits.com

Silk City Fibers
155 Oxford St.
Paterson, NJ 07522
silkcityfibers.com

Skacel
PO Box 88110
Seattle, WA 98138
skacelknitting.com

SweetGeorgia Yarns, Inc
110-408 E. Kent Ave. S.
Vancouver, BC
Canada V5X 2X7
sweetgeorgiayarns.com

Tahki-Stacy Charles, Inc./
Filatura Di Crosa
70-60 83rd St., Bldg. 12
Glendale, NY 11385
tahkistacycharles.com

Trendsetter Yarns
16745 Saticoy St., Ste. 101
Van Nuys, CA 91406
trendsetteryarns.com

Universal Yarn
5991 Caldwell Business
Park Dr.
Harrisburg, NC 28075
universalyarn.com

WEBS/Valley Fibers
6 Industrial Pkwy.
Easthampton, MA 01027
yarn.com

Looms courtesy of:

Schacht Spindle Co., Inc.
6101 Ben Pl.
Boulder, CO 80301
schachtspindle.com

**Source for Yarn to Yards
Balance:**

Eugene Textile Center
1510 Jacobs Dr.
Eugene, OR 97402
eugenetextilecenter.com

INDEX

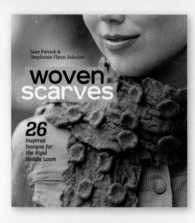